Shona Women in Zimbabwe—A Purchased People?

# afRican cHRistian studies seRies (afRics)

This series will make available significant works in the field of African Christian studies, taking into account the many forms of Christianity across the whole continent of Africa. African Christian studies is defined here as any scholarship that relates to themes and issues on the history, nature, identity, character, and place of African Christianity in world Christianity. It also refers to topics that address the continuing search for abundant life for Africans through multiple appeals to African religions and African Christianity in a challenging social context. The books in this series are expected to make significant contributions in historicizing trends in African Christian studies, while shifting the contemporary discourse in these areas from narrow theological concerns to a broader inter-disciplinary engagement with African religio-cultural traditions and Africa's challenging social context.

The series will cater to scholarly and educational texts in the areas of religious studies, theology, mission studies, biblical studies, philosophy, social justice, and other diverse issues current in African Christianity. We define these studies broadly and specifically as primarily focused on new voices, fresh perspectives, new approaches, and historical and cultural analyses that are emerging because of the significant place of African Christianity and African religio-cultural traditions in world Christianity. The series intends to continually fill a gap in African scholarship, especially in the areas of social analysis in African Christian studies, African philosophies, new biblical and narrative hermeneutical approaches to African theologies, and the challenges facing African women in today's Africa and within African Christianity. Other diverse themes in African Traditional Religions; African ecology; African ecclesiology; inter-cultural, inter-ethnic, and inter-religious dialogue; ecumenism; creative inculturation; African theologies of development, reconciliation, globalization, and poverty reduction will also be covered in this series.

SERIES EDITORS

Dr. Stan Chu Ilo (DePaul University, Chicago, USA)

Dr. Esther Acolatse (Duke University, Durham, USA)

Dr. Mwenda Ntarangwi (Calvin College, Grand Rapids, MI, USA)

# Shona Women in Zimbabwe
# —A Purchased People?

## Marriage, Bridewealth, Domestic Violence, and the Christian Traditions on Women

JOHN CHITAKURE

PICKWICK *Publications* · Eugene, Oregon

SHONA WOMEN IN ZIMBABWE—A PURCHASED PEOPLE?
Marriage, Bridewealth, Domestic Violence, and the Christian Traditions on Women

African Christian Studies Series 12

Pickwick Publications
An Imprint of Wipf and Stock Publishers
199 W. 8th Ave., Suite 3
Eugene, OR 97401

www.wipfandstock.com

PAPERBACK ISBN: 978-1-4982-9305-1
HARDCOVER ISBN: 978-1-4982-9307-5
EBOOK ISBN: 978-1-4982-9306-8

### *Cataloguing-in-Publication data:*

Names: Chitakure, John.

Title: Shona women in Zimbabwe—a purchased people? : marriage, bridewealth, domestic violence, and the Christian traditions on women / John Chikature.

Description: Eugene, OR : Pickwick Publications, 2016 | African Christian Studies Series | Includes bibliographical references and index.

Identifiers: ISBN 978-1-4982-9305-1 (paperback) | ISBN 978-1-4982-9307-5 (hardcover) | ISBN 978-1-4982-9306-8 (ebook)

Subjects: LCSH: Shona (African people)—Religion.| Women in Christianity—Africa. | Christianity—Zimbabwe. | Shona (African people)—Women.

Classification: BR1360 .C45 2016 (paperback) | BR1360 .C45 (ebook)

Manufactured in the U.S.A.          09/19/16

To my mother, Mapfumbudza Chitakure, my mother-in-law, Ozalia Ngongoni Shumbairerwa, and all other survivors of domestic violence.

*A man who teaches his son to use violence in resolving relational differences with other people, is also preparing him to use the same violence in his own home to suppress the voices of his mother, wife, sisters, and daughters. Anybody who wants to establish sustainable world peace should start by eradicating domestic violence in his own home.*

# Contents

Mashonaland West

Mashonaland Central

Harare

Matabeleland North

Mashonaland East

Midlands

Manicaland

Bulawayo

Matabeleland South

Masvingo

Map was done by Nyasha Theobald Chitakure

**Map of Zimbabwe: Provinces**

Tunisia
Morocco
Algeria
Libya
Egypt
Burkina
Faso
Mauritaina Mali
Niger
Chad
Sudan
Togo
Senegal
Nigeria
Ethiopia
Southern
Sudan
Uganda
Cen. Afr. Rep.
Somalia
Guinea
Ghana
Dem.
Rep. of
Congo
Rwanda
Burundi
Tanzania
Kenya
Liberia
Benin
Malawi
Siera
Leone
Cameroon
Angola
Zambia
Madagascar
Namibia
Botswana
Cote
D'ivore
Congo
Gabon
South Africa
Mozambique
Equatorial
Guinea
Swaziland
**Zimbabwe**
Map was done by Mufaro Sean Chitakure
Lesotho

**Map of Africa**

# Preface

BRIDEWEALTH IS THE COMPENSATION that the bridegroom pays to the father or family of the woman that he intends to marry or is married to that legitimates the union, gives him paternal rights over their offspring, awards him exclusive sexual rights over the woman, and a complete access to her productive capacity. This compensation is paid in the form of money, cattle, food, clothes, and any other items that might be deemed appropriate by the family of the bride. Bridewealth is a practice that is found in many Bantu-speaking African states such as Zambia, Malawi, Zimbabwe, Namibia, South Africa, Mozambique, Tanzania, Kenya, Lesotho, Swaziland, Nigeria, among others. However, it should be noted that there are variations in the way the phenomenon is practiced by different ethnic groups. The form of bridewealth that has been explored in this book is practiced in Zimbabwe by the Shona people, particularly the Karanga of Masvingo Province. Although the crux of bridewealth is the same among all Shona ethnic groups, each family, village, or clan may practice it differently because there are no legal guidelines as to how it should be performed. Therefore, it becomes difficult to generalize about it. The bridewealth practice is dynamic and several aspects that have become part of it have been borrowed from other Shona ethnic groups.

Zimbabwe is a landlocked country that is located in Southern Africa bordering South Africa, in the south, Botswana in the west, Zambia in the north, and Mozambique in the east. Zimbabwe has a population of about fourteen million people some of whom live in the diaspora. The country was a colony of Britain for almost a hundred years, and it got its independence from Britain in 1980. Zimbabwe was formerly known as Rhodesia, named after Cecil John Rhodes (1853–1902), a wealthy magnate who obtained a concession from King Lobengula of the Ndebele people in 1888, to occupy the country from South Africa. Armed with the Rudd Concession, the Pioneer Column, which was founded and funded by Cecil John Rhodes, occupied Zimbabwe in 1890. Rhodes did not live long to enjoy the fruits of his labors; he died in South Africa, at the age of forty-two and was buried in Zimbabwe on the Matopos Hills, near the city of Bulawayo. During the federation of Rhodesia and Nyasaland (1953–1963), the country became Southern Rhodesia. In 1979, from June 1 to December 12, it became Zimbabwe–Rhodesia after Bishop Abel Tendekai Muzorewa won the general elections, which were boycotted by other nationalists such as Robert Mugabe and Dr. Joshua Nkomo.

There are two major ethnic groups in Zimbabwe—the Shona and the Ndebele. The Shona are the majority and constitute about 82 percent of the population. The Ndebele constitute about 16 percent of the population. Other ethnic groups including Whites represent about 2 percent of the population. Although some ethnographers argue that the Shona are not the indigenous people of Zimbabwe, they have been in the country longer, and it would be logical to count them among the earliest inhabitants of the country. The Ndebele arrived from South Africa in 1838 and 1840, under the leadership of King Mzilikazi (c. 1790–1868) who led the Khumalo northwards under the pursuit of King Shaka of the Zulu. King Mzilikazi was succeeded by his son, Lobengula (1845–1894), as the King of the Ndebele people, around 1870. King Lobengula is believed to have died in 1894 at the end of the Anglo-Ndebele War of 1893–94, and there is no agreement concerning the location of his burial place. Under both kings, the Ndebele defeated and continued to raid some of the Shona people who lived around the area in which they resettled. The Shona include ethnical groups such as the Zezuru, Korekore, Karanga, Ndau, and Manyika. Both the Ndebele and Shona practice bridewealth. As has been said above, this book does not claim to speak for all Shona people because there are many variations in the way bridewealth is negotiated. I write it from the perspective of the Karanga people of Masvingo, under chief Nyajena. However, most of the issues explored here are relevant to most Shona clans and groups.

Since this book started as my doctoral project in 2008, at the Catholic Theological Union, at Chicago, it is not surprising that some of the things that are mentioned might have been overtaken by time but are still relevant to the topic. For instance, Pope John Paul II is now a Saint. Be that as it may, two things that have remained unchanged are domestic violence and bridewealth. I do not claim to be an expert on these issues, but I hope to contribute to the debate. It should be noted that bridewealth payments have been privatized, and consequently, there are many variations in the manner of the negotiations and the amount charged.

San Antonio, Texas, USA, 2016

# Acknowledgments

THIS BOOK IS A result of the reworking and expansion of my doctoral thesis that I submitted to the Catholic Theological Union at Chicago in 2008 as a partial fulfillment of the Doctor of Ministry degree that was awarded to me in May of the same year. When I think of the many people who did support me throughout the process, the first two who come to my mind are Prof. Anthony Gittins and Prof. Edward Foley, my two supervisors, who worked so diligently to facilitate the birthing of this project.

A very special word of gratitude should go to the CTU Bernardin Center for awarding me a scholarship that enabled me to pursue my doctoral studies. Another special word of thanks should go to the Franciscan Friars of Saint Peter's Catholic Church, in the Loop, who offered me food and board for free throughout the period of my studies. I would like all of them to know that I would not have come to the CTU to study theology had it not been for their kindness, love, and generosity. I also thank Dr. Robstein Chidavaenzi for reviewing this work and the valuable comments that he offered.

Finally, I would like to thank members of my family who assisted me in one way or the other. My mother, Mapfumbudza, played a very special role in this writing because it was her story that inspired me. My wife, Blessing's contribution was significant. She worked so hard and looked after the kids while I was away studying. The thought and love of our children, Nyasha, and Mufaro, never ceased to propel me to work harder. To those members of my extended family that I have not mentioned by names, I thank you all.

# Abbreviations

CTU      Catholic Theological Union

RCC      Roman Catholic Church

ZCBC      Zimbabwe Catholic Bishops Conference

USCCB      United States Conference of Catholic Bishops

SCC      Small Christian Communities

EFZ      Evangelical Fellowship of Zimbabwe

ZCC      Zimbabwe Council of Churches

NGO      Non- Governmental Organization

STIs      Sexual Transmitted Infections

IMBISA      The Inter-Regional Meeting of Bishops of Southern Africa

HIV      Human Immunodeficiency Virus

AIDS      Acquired Immunodeficiency Syndrome

AMECEA      Association of Member Episcopal Conferences of Eastern Africa

# Introduction

MY FATHER WAS A heavyweight boxing champion and had an insatiable passion for the game. Within the first round of the fight, he would make sure that his enemy was knocked down two or three times in a row. Unlike professional boxers, my father had no rules governing him; he had no referee, and consequently, he would not stop boxing his pleading opponent, despite the pleas and cries for mercy from the opponent, and the scared and unwilling spectators. He kicked, shoved, slapped, punched, arm-twisted, thrashed, and cursed the half-dead opponent. The *great* fighter in him would not stop until the enemy passed out, or pretended to be so. He could have become the world heavyweight boxing champion, but unfortunately or, fortunately, he never challenged and never had any other opponents but one—my mother. She was an easy opponent for him because he knew that he would never lose the fight since she never fought back. I do not know why she never fought back. It could have been out of her respect for a brute who had fathered her four children or the result of the crippling and petrifying power of his brutality.

My brother and I would stand there crying helplessly, witnessing the brutality of a pseudo-fighter in its totality. I was about four years old, but my mother's tears remain vivid and fresh in my mind. I still remember how my mother, brother, and I would then go to some church or community hall, in the middle of the night and would sleep there on the veranda. Sometimes my mom would knock on the church door, even though she knew that the door was locked and that there was no one living there. Probably she thought that God would open the door for us miraculously, or perhaps it was merely the confused action of a battered, dehumanized, and humiliated woman.

That was around the year 1977 in the small mining compound of Mashava, in Zimbabwe. My mother is lucky to be a survivor of domestic violence because God intervened. Yes, he sometimes does. My father just disappeared around 1977, never to be seen again. My mother is still alive, but she still bears the marks of the brutal attacks she endured stoically—she partially lost her hearing. In our family, we never mention my father, and whenever his name is mentioned accidentally, a current of pain passes between my mother and those of us who witnessed the atrocities of a heavy-weight boxing champion who never was.

Most women who lived during my mom's time would agree with me that my mother was not alone in her tribulations. Many other women were treated much the same way by their husbands. My mother's trials ended in 1977, but sadly domestic violence continues worldwide. With the spread of globalization and the conversion of many people to Christianity and other religious traditions, people erroneously thought that domestic violence would eventually just disappear since it is against the principles of the gospel of Jesus Christ, the spirit of civilization, and the Golden Rule. It didn't. Domestic violence is one of the crimes against humanity that continue to bedevil the human society in general and the Shona society in particular, despite the presence of Christianity and other religious traditions. In fact, some specific religious practices contribute to the subordination of women in some religions. Among the Shona of Zimbabwe, one of the contributing factors to the systematic subordination of wives to their husbands is the payment of commercialized and privatized bridewealth. This factor will be explored in detail in chapter 3. But can women be liberated from domestic violence and some cultural practices that proliferate it? Can governments and Christians assist in the restoration of women's dignity, humanity, and emancipation?

In 2006, about thirty-one years after I witnessed the abuse of my mother by my own father, the government of Zimbabwe passed into law the Domestic Violence Act [Chapter 5:16] that seeks to address the plight of abused women by arresting and sending their abusers to jail for a period not to exceed ten years.[1] The controversial debates that took place in Parliament when the Act was under discussion show how some Zimbabwean men view women. A good example of this was a male legislator who categorically and blasphemously argued as follows: "I stand here representing God Almighty. Women are not equal to men. It is a dangerous Bill and let it be known in Zimbabwe that the right, privilege, and status of men are gone. I stand here alone and say this Bill must not be passed in this house. It is a diabolic Bill. Our powers are being usurped in daylight in this house."[2] Although some

---

1. *Domestic Violence Act* [Chapter 5:16], No. 14/2006, became law in Zimbabwe on October 25, 2007.

2. This was said in the House of Parliament in 2006 by Timothy Mabhawu, a member of Parliament for the Movement for Democratic Change (MDC) for Mabvuku, during a heated debate on the Domestic Violence Bill. He was later suspended by his party for that utterance.

Zimbabweans condemned the legislator, he still had sympathizers. It was disturbing to see how both God and the devil were brought into the debate.

Now, over a decade after the inception of that law, Zimbabweans are still waiting to witness the fruits of the law and some people already fear that the law might not change the situation of the violated women of Zimbabwe because of several reasons. First, unemployed victims of domestic violence may refuse to report domestic violence to law enforcement agents because the victims stand to lose more if the abusive husbands are incarcerated especially in families in which the perpetrator is the sole bread winner. Second, there is fear that the law may cause more harm than good since it may lead to more divorces at a time when most Zimbabwean women still rely on their husbands economically. Third, some people have repeatedly argued that what domestic violence survivors want is not the arrest of the perpetrators but the stopping of domestic violence. Writing from a different perspective, Rebecca P. Sewall, Arati Vasan, and others have given an analysis that may apply to the Zimbabwe situation. According to them, women want violence to stop, not their husbands sent to jail. Women prefer therapy and re-education rather than punishment.[3] Civil remedies are more preferable than prosecution.

If people are to take the re-education of both perpetrators and victims of domestic violence as a way to fight domestic violence, then all the Christian churches in Zimbabwe become of paramount importance. By virtue of their prophetic calling, Christian churches have the God-given duty to preach against all kinds of oppression of human beings by fellow humans, irrespective of their gender, race, color, and nationality. Although some churches in Zimbabwe, for example, the Roman Catholic Church, have spoken boldly against other kinds of human oppression and injustice, they have not categorically and openly spoken against domestic violence. When writing against political intolerance in Zimbabwe, the Zimbabwe Catholic Bishops Conference (ZCBC), the Evangelical Fellowship of Zimbabwe (EFZ), and the Zimbabwe Council of Churches (ZCC) rightly stipulated that "the Church is a divine institution in the world, comprising men and women called to serve God and humanity through the preaching of a liberating Gospel and service to alleviate human suffering in this world. As a religious organization the church embraces the vast majority of the people of Zimbabwe. It is closest to the people. They trust their religious leadership and we can claim to know their desires and aspirations better than any other organization."[4]

3. Sewall et al., eds., *State Responses to Domestic Violence*, 7.
4. ZCBC, EFZ, and ZCC, *The Zimbabwe We Want*, 12–13.

The above quotation leaves no question as to whether the Christian churches in general and the Roman Catholic Church, in particular, have the mandate to deal with issues bedeviling the Zimbabwean society. What Christian churches need is comprehensive support so that they may fully exercise their prophetic duty of preaching against any violence against women. Zimbabwean women need to be emancipated from all the abuse that they suffer from their spouses.

What makes me think that I have a duty to advocate for the emancipation of Shona women? First, I was born and raised in a society where domestic violence was rampant. As a young boy, I witnessed several men battering their wives. Some of the victims and perpetrators were related to me. Second, I read about domestic violence in Zimbabwe's daily newspapers. In almost every major daily newspaper in Zimbabwe, there is a sad story of an abused woman. Third, as a high school teacher I had the privilege of counseling students. Some of my clients told me that their fathers abused their mothers, and some were even afraid to return home for the vacation because they would again witness the violent situations between their parents. Whenever I listen to stories of domestic violence, I am reminded of my childhood and the suffering of my mother who was a victim of spousal abuse in much the same way.

To what extent can resources of religious tradition and the Shona cultural heritage provide both negative and positive resources in the proliferation and fight against domestic violence among the Shona of Zimbabwe? I strongly think that the Christian churches have the resources, authority, and mandate to address the issue of domestic violence. They do have the pulpit and a willing audience that includes both victims and perpetrators of domestic violence. People who go to church are looking for inner transformation, and most of them are willing to walk an extra mile to achieve whatever they aspire to achieve. What churches need to do is to begin.

Several reasons have been put forward to explain the existence of domestic violence among the Shona of Zimbabwe. Although a variety of causes of domestic violence will be addressed briefly, this work is more focused on how the practice of bridewealth contributes to the subjugation, oppression, demeaning, and abuse of some women by their spouses in Zimbabwe. Unless the issue of bridewealth is addressed, the complete emancipation of Zimbabwean women that some people tirelessly work for will remain unattainable. Of course, in the political arena significant achievements in gender representation have been achieved but in the home, the emancipation of women still demands a lot to be done.

I have three basic assumptions in undertaking this project. First, among the Shona of Zimbabwe, it is usually the wife who is abused by the husband, although there are rare cases in which husbands are victims of domestic abuse by their wives. There have been reports of such situations, but they are not the norm of the Shona society. The Shona cultural practice of bridewealth, particularly in its present corrupted form, among other cultural practices, makes wives subordinate to their husbands, and this usually leads to wife abuse.

Second, both men and women were created in the image of God, and because of that, both deserve to be treated with dignity and respect. Neither men nor women have the right to take advantage of the physical weakness of the other, to oppress the other. What men want their wives to do for them, they should also be ready to do for their wives. The Golden Rule should be applied.

Third, I also assume that marriage and the children, who are the fruits of most marriages, are crucial to the Shona and Christians. Anything that threatens the safety and sanity of the men, women, children, and the integrity of the institution of marriage in the way that domestic violence does, must be given serious deliberation and condemnation by all Christians.

Fourth, domestic violence is evil. It dehumanizes, hurts, and humiliates the victim. It takes away the love that should reside in families. It brings mistrust, hatred, and anger. It causes divorce. Domestic violence also affects the children who witness it as much as it affects the victim. It creates fear in the victim and the children who are in most cases, the unwilling spectators.

My final assumption is that Christians have the authority and spiritual responsibility to challenge domestic violence and to lead men to behavioral change, which will recognize and respect the dignity and rights of women. The Christian churches have the resources to educate women as to the importance of fighting for equal rights by raising women to higher positions in churches' administrative bodies so that they have a say in the implementation of programs that support the well-being of both women and children.

I must admit right from the onset that I have my limitations in discussing women subjugation in Zimbabwe. First, I am an outsider concerning the subjugation of women in the sense that I am a man trying to enter the world of dominated, battered, subjugated, exploited, and oppressed women. Second, the perpetrators of domestic violence are mostly men. So, by association, I am already a perpetrator of domestic violence. My suggestions might be considered to be tantamount to shading crocodile tears. Third, the cultural practice of bridewealth that I intend to challenge is a very widespread and deep-rooted practice, and I know that some men and women might disagree with my perspectives and suggestions. I strongly think that those disagreements will ignite a debate that will give people an opportunity to revisit the cultural practice of bridewealth. Finally, domestic violence is a clandestine crime that happens between people who have deep love feelings for each other. It is a crime between intimate individuals and because of that, it occurs within closed doors. To worsen the matter, some victims try to cover up for their perpetrators for one reason or another. But, whether we physically witness it or not, domestic violence is ubiquitous.

Despite all the above challenges, I go ahead and write about domestic violence and how bridewealth is one of the factors that contributes to its proliferation. Why do I bother? I am of the conviction that unless bridewealth is challenged, regulated and probably abolished, the talk of Shona women emancipation will remain a farce. If anyone is serious about eradicating domestic violence, he or she must attack its root causes. Yes, I am concerned because I too am the son of my mother; a woman who has a story to tell, but has no means to do it. This story is my mother's story, my mother's call, and I tell it with both pride and shame. I am ashamed because my own father was the perpetrator and I am proud because I can write about it on behalf of my mother, who could have told it from an experiential perspective had her father empowered her with education, but he did not.

The methodology I use in this book is mainly derived from the Whiteheads. It has a model and a method that come into conversation time and again. The model has three parts namely, religious tradition, experience, and the surrounding culture. The process includes attending, which means the getting of information by careful and empathetic listening to battered women's personal experiences.[5] Assertion follows and calls for a dialogue between the battered women's experiences, culture and religious tradition. The dialogue will then lead to a pastoral response.

## Description of Chapters

Chapter 1 deals with the statistics of domestic violence in the world in general, and in Zimbabwe in particular. It then explores the terms that are used to refer to domestic violence and will pinpoint the words that this book will use. It also deals with the causes and types of domestic violence while pointing out briefly that the payment of bridewealth contributes to domestic violence in Zimbabwe, to a larger extent. Finally, the chapter deals with the same old question: why do abused women stay?

The domestic violence that this book discusses happens within the various types of Shona marriages. Chapter 2 explores the Shona types of marriages some of which are no longer in existence now. The chapter's primary thesis is that every kind of the Shona marriage determines the manner

5. Whitehead and Whitehead, *Method in Ministry,* 3–17.

in which bridewealth talks are carried out. Consequently, the nature of marriage may ascertain the size of the bridewealth to be charged and how and when it is paid. Those types of marriage that give the parents of the bride more leverage in bridewealth negotiations are considered more esteemed, and those types in which bridewealth has not been paid, are not recognized as marriages until bridewealth is paid.

Among the Shona, the payment of bridewealth legitimates a marriage, and no purported marriage is a marriage until bridewealth negotiations begin. Although the majority of Zimbabweans believe that bridewealth is one of their cultural and religious practices that should not be discarded, chapter 3 argues that it is one of the leading causes of the subjugation, oppression, exploitation, and abuse of Shona women by their husbands. This chapter discusses the meaning of a Shona marriage and the kinship system in which marriages take place. It also explores the rationale for the payment of bridewealth. The chapter goes on to discuss the rights that the husband gets after paying bridewealth. Wives do not get the same rights because they do not pay bridewealth. Some of those rights tend to be against the welfare of women. The thesis of this chapter is that bridewealth is the primary cultural cause of the abuse of Shona women by their husbands and that the emancipation of Shona women will remain an unattainable dream unless bridewealth is revisited, regularized or even abolished. But are Shona people ready to discard bridewealth?

Chapter 4 traces how the Christian tradition, particularly the Roman Catholic Church, has viewed women right from the time of Jesus. Although most Christian churches agree that women and men were created in the image of God, they do not entirely agree concerning the degree to which men and women should be treated as equals. Many Christian churches condemn violence against women but very few, if any, have tried to challenge cultural practices that support the subjugation of women such as the payment of exorbitant bridewealth. Among the Shona, the majority of Christians openly condone the practice. There are very few Christian groups especially some African Independent Churches, and those of European descent that are either indifferent or do not practice or support it.

Chapter 4 has five sections, and each section has three parts. The sections are as follows: (1) Jesus' attitude towards women in the Gospel of Luke; (2) Paul on women and marriage; (3) Tertullian on women and marriage; (4) Pope John Paul II on women, marriage, and domestic violence; (5) and the Zimbabwe Catholic Bishops' Conference on women, family, and violence. The first part of each section explores the positive teachings and views on marriage and women in the selected aspect of the Roman Catholic Church tradition. The second part of each section deals with the negative attitudes and teachings that have tended to look upon women, as inferior to men, and upon married life as inferior to celibacy and chastity. Although the Roman Catholic Church tradition is used in this chapter, most Christian churches have not been so supportive of Shona women with regards to the payment of bridewealth.

Chapter 5 deals with the conversation between human experience, culture, and religious tradition. It uses the James D. Whitehead and Evelyn Eaton Whitehead's methodology of theological reflection and then apply the method to domestic violence among the Shona. The chapter will try to tap into the Shona culture and Christian tradition for ways by which the Shona women of Zimbabwe can be emancipated.

Chapter 6 includes the recommendations to pastors on how to liberate women in their congregations from patriarchal dominance. It suggests pastoral strategies that may be helpful in the restoration of the dignity of Shona women and the fight against domestic violence in Zimbabwe and elsewhere.

# Chapter 1

## Domestic Violence
## Nomenclature, Causes, and Types

### Introduction

DOMESTIC VIOLENCE IS UBIQUITOUS although some societies and cultures may experience more of it than others. The forms it takes and the degree to, and the frequency at which it is practiced might differ, but it remains domestic violence—ugly, uncivilized, and inhuman. Its occurrence might not be so evident and publicized in some societies, but that does not make it non-existent. That is why it is naïve and myopic to think that some human societies are free from gender violence. In the past, some activists thought that gender-based violence was a crime of the uneducated and uncivilized nations of the world, but that notion has been challenged and disapproved by the empirical evidence that comes from several cross-cultural victims' experiences. The United Nations has observed that "Violence against women is both universal and particular. It is universal in that there is no region of the world, no country and no culture in which women's freedom from violence has been secured."[1]

According to Terry Davidson, the problem of domestic violence is as old as humanity itself, and it has no ethnic, cultural, religious or social class boundaries, and it is as ubiquitous as the air that we breathe.[2] For many

1. United Nations, *Violence against Women*, 28.
2. Davidson, *Conjugal Crime*, 1.

9

years in the history of humanity, domestic violence went on unchallenged because most societies considered it part of human life. In some areas of the world, it was only recognized as a social problem in the seventies.[3] Before that, many societies believed that it was right to discipline one's wife by beating. According to Richard J. Gelles, "Throughout history there have been legal and cultural precedents which, to a degree, sanctioned the right of a husband to use violence on his wife."[4]

Although domestic violence may not seem to exist, it is a reality for some women. It fakes its death, and it may be successful in doing so because most of it goes unchecked due to the secrecy that surrounds its commission. Margaret M. Leddy observes that wife battering is a silent crime, rarely reported in most societies because of the ignorance and denial of both victims and perpetrators.[5] The Professional Education Taskforce on Family Violence affirms the observation that other scholars have asserted that domestic violence remains undetected because of the pain and humiliation it instills in the victims and also the lack of evidence and witnesses that characterizes its occurrence.[6]

Domestic violence takes various forms and degrees of severity depending on the geographical location of the community in which it is perpetrated and the caliber of the couple involved. In some countries where gender-based violence has been outlawed, it tends to appear in subtle ways to evade detection by members of the public and the law enforcement agents. In societies where very little has been done to eradicate it, domestic violence happens out in the open, in more vivid and despicable ways.

This chapter starts by giving brief descriptions of some terms that are related to and can be used interchangeably with domestic violence. The chapter then goes on to describe briefly different forms of domestic violence. It finally gives statistics of domestic violence among the Shona of Zimbabwe and elsewhere. Although gender-based violence can appear in various forms and contexts, and can be perpetrated by either men or women, this chapter deals with the violence that is directed towards women by men in civil, customary, and unregistered marriages. Some writers have called this type of domestic violence, marital violence, which I think sufficiently captures the spirit of what this chapter is all about.

---

3. Gelles, *Family Violence*, 106.
4. Ibid.
5. Leddy, "Domestic Violence," 1.
6. Professional Education Taskforce on Family Violence, *Family Violence,* 65.

## Terminological Issues

### Domestic Violence

Kathleen Waits has defined domestic as "a criminal act of assault, sexual assault, sexual battery, or other act that injures or kills a family or household member by another who is or was residing in the same single dwelling unit."[7] In the same manner, the Zimbabwe *Domestic Violence Act* [Chapter 5:16], No. 14/2006, defines domestic violence as, "Any unlawful act, omission or behavior which results in death or direct infliction of physical, sexual or mental injury to any complainant by a respondent and includes the following: physical abuse, sexual abuse, emotional, verbal and psychological, economic abuse; intimidation, harassment, stalking . . . "[8] Domestic violence can be violence directed at a child, husband, wife, brother, sister, and so on, within the framework of a family.

### Gender-based Violence

The gender-based violence is committed within a family set up, usually by any family member against another family member. Sometimes people commit it using a weapon such as a knife, gun, stone, stick, and so on. In most countries, gender-based violence is more directed towards women than men. This scenario can be a result of the physical, biological differences between men and women. Although there are men who are victims of gender-based violence in Zimbabwe, most of the victims are female. Several reasons have contributed to that scenario. First, most men are biologically and physically stronger than most women, so, when it comes to matters of fighting, men seem to have the upper hand. Second, in the past, Zimbabwean women were not as educated as men, and they tended to stay at home looking after the children while men pursued education and gainful employment in industries and towns. So, when it comes to economic power, more men are better placed than women. Third, some people argue that women are more peace-loving than men. So, most women are committed to promoting peace in the family. In the traditional Shona family, even if a woman is physically stronger than her husband, she may not subject him to any physical violence because of respect. Of course, some women have been reported to abuse their husbands, but that is an exception to the norm.

---

7. Waits, *Battered Women and Their Children*, 1998.
8. *Zimbabwe Domestic Violence Act.*

*Victim or Survivor*

Another terminological issue concerns the use of words *victim* and *survivor* in connection with domestic violence. It seems that the word victim refers to the person who is in the process of being victimized although the violence might be intermittent. A survivor is someone who has lived through domestic violence and has managed to extricate oneself from the violent person and environment. Although the two words are sometimes used interchangeably, they have somewhat different meanings. Some think that the word survivor is a more positive and empowering term than the word victim that seems to have some connotation of presenting the abused person as being a mere passive sufferer. It should be noted that a person who has survived domestic violence may sometimes be victimized again by the same perpetrator or a different one. It is also true that victimization does not end with the physical act of abuse but it may continue in the memory of the survivor long after the abuse. If the survivor sustained physical marks as a result of the abuse, these may act as reminders of the traumatic events to the survivor. It seems that a battered person goes through a simultaneous process of victimization and surviving. Hence, one person can identify with both terms.

*Marital Violence*

Marital violence refers to the violence that happens between people who will, are, and might be married. These people might be cohabiting rather than married in the strictest sense of the word. Usually, the violence is directed against women although there are men who are also victimized by their wives in every culture and country. The focus is on the woman because she is considered to be the weaker partner, physically, and in most Zimbabwe cases, women are economically marginalized. In marital violence, children are also caught in the crossfire as either passive or active spectators of the violence that happens in the family. According to Lundy Bancroft, "5 million children per year witness an assault on their mothers, an experience that can leave them traumatized."[9] So, marital violence happens within the framework of marriage. It should be borne in mind that marriage means different things in different cultures. The Zimbabwean law recognizes both customary and civil marriages as legitimate. This book will use the term domestic violence and marital violence interchangeably to refer to the violence that is perpetrated against women within the framework of marriage.

9. Bancroft, *Why Does He Do That?*, 8.

## Violence against Women

Violence against women is the abuse that is directed at women, in general. This kind of violence can happen to any woman either within the confines of a marriage or outside. Nancy A. Crowell and Ann W. Burgess define violence against women as ". . . a wide range of acts, including murder, rape and sexual assault, physical assault, emotional abuse, battering, stalking, prostitution, genital mutilation, sexual harassment, and pornography."[10] This form of violence is usually perpetrated by men although there are also women who abuse other women. This kind of violence does not spare even young girls who are sometimes forced into child marriages, sex slavery, and prostitution. It can be perpetrated in the name of religion or culture. In Africa, there are ethnic groups that practice circumcision of women, a practice that has become notoriously known as genital mutilation. This ritual has been outlawed in most countries, but, like any other banned religious practice, it survives secretly. Those who practice it believe and argue that it is part of their cultural and religious heritage and because of that it should not be discarded. There is also forced marriages of young girls who can hardly give their marital consents because they are minors.

## Family Violence

Family violence happens within the framework of the familial relationships. First, it occurs within the nucleus family. It can be a husband who abuses his wife or children. It can also refer to the woman who may do the same to either the husband or the children or even both. Sometimes this type of violence is only directed towards children. In every culture, people have acceptable ways of disciplining children, and most people know when some form of punishment has gone beyond what is considered reasonable and acceptable within a particular culture. This violence may include beating up the children, denying them food, clothes, school fees, accommodation, forcing them to work, neglecting them, rape, and so on. Either the mother or father or both can perpetrate violence against their own children.

Second, family violence can be committed by the extended family members or against members of the extended family. In some communities, children are raped by people who are related to them such as uncles, aunts, nephews, nieces, stepbrothers, and stepfathers. Such abusers have an easy access to the vulnerable children because they are trusted by both the

---

10. Crowell and Burgess, *Understanding Violence against Women*, 9.

children their parents. Sometimes such abusers are legal guardians of the victims.

Third, among the Shona people of Zimbabwe, the extended family is of significant importance. There are instances where brothers of the husband can assault their brother's wife. The Shona culture permits that because they too are considered the husbands of the victim. In some cases, such abuse becomes acute when the man dies leaving a widow. There are instances where relatives of the deceased husband have confiscated the property that has been left by the dead man leaving the widow and her children empty handed.

## Observation

When writers and activists use any of the above terms, they usually refer to violence against women. Most writers are aware of some violence that is committed against men, but they argue that that is not the norm in most communities. Men abuse women because they are physically stronger than females and in most societies, men are socialized to use violence.[11] So, all men are potential abusers of women, and that makes it more difficult for the plight of battered men to find sympathizers. Most people do not care much about abused men because they erroneously think that it is their fault and weakness that cause their abuse.

## Causes of Domestic Violence

### Low Self-esteem

Low self-esteem affects both men and women who are involved in an abusive marriage. A person who suffers from low self-esteem feels inadequate, insecure, and worthless.[12] In men, it can be caused by the type of job one works or the lack of it. If he has a job, the abusive man might be comparing his salary or job with that of other people particularly, relatives, friends or neighbors. Such a man may end up thinking that other people are better than him because they have better jobs, houses, salaries, cars, clothes, and other properties than him. So, the man compensates what he lacks by proving to himself and the world that although he is worthless, in the eyes of his friends, relatives, and neighbors, there is something that he can do to prove

11. Jacobson and Gottan, *When Men Batter Women*, 35.
12. Kakar, *Domestic Abuse, Public Policy / Criminal Justice*, 132.

his worthiness. In some cases, some men think that by abusing their wives, they are, in fact, showing the world that they are *real men*.

The abused woman's low-esteem might be seen in her persistence in remaining in an abusive relationship although there could be other alternatives. Some of those women may think that their husbands beat them up because they are ugly, undesirable, disgraceful, headstrong, incorrigible, pugnacious, and troublesome. Such a woman might conclude that if she gets divorced by the violent husband her chances of getting another marriage partner might be very slim. Sometimes a violent man gets to know about the low self-esteem of the wife and usually takes advantage of that. After the abuse, the husband may remind the abused woman of her freedom to leave if she wants to. The same man might tell her that no other man would love and marry her because of her incorrigibility. The abusive man wants the woman to believe that he is doing her a favor by continuing to stay with her despite her shortcomings. A woman who firmly believes in her husband's affirmation of her beauty will feel that she is ugly, evil, headstrong, incorrigible, and worthless because her husband says so.

In some cases, a man reinforces the abusive wife's feelings of low self-esteem if he knows the economic hardships that his wife's relatives experience. In that case, the woman is reminded that her parents are poor and that she has nowhere to go if she decides to leave him. She is also told that she should be grateful to have a husband who gives her food, clothes, and a house. Some abusive men try to appear very generous to the relatives of the woman. They spoil them with gifts and pay school fees for some of them. The violent husband makes them depend on him. By so doing, the wife is isolated, and her relatives might not believe her if she were to tell them about her ordeal with the husband.

If a man knows about his wife's not-so-rose the past, he might regularly refer to it during quarrels to humiliate and embarrass her. Abusive husbands usually refer to that embarrassing past to diminish the little self-esteem that the wife still has. The abuser's argument goes like this: "You have a filthy past. There are better women out there, and I can get any of them if I want. You have to put up with any treatment that I deem necessary because you are worthless." Unfortunately, some women tend to believe that rhetoric.

In other cases, low self-esteem is caused by one of the spouses having less education than the other. If the husband is less educated than the wife, he might want to compensate what he lacks by abusing the woman. If the woman is less educated than the husband, she might be reminded every time that they have an argument that she is not educated, and, therefore, worthless. In Zimbabwe, there are cases where educated men compel their spouses who do not possess Ordinary Level certificates to go back to high school. Going back to high school might be the right thing to do if the woman makes the decision to do so. It becomes a form of domestic violence if the wife is compelled to do so by the husband so that he may boost his ego among his friends or workmates. Sometimes such women have to attend the high schools where their husbands teach, and if they fail to keep up with the expectations of the teachers, it demeans the women. If they fail their examinations as some of them do, then, they become the laughing stock, not only of their husbands but also to conventional students. That severely diminishes a woman's self-esteem. Men who are not abusive to their wives, do not arbitrarily send their wives back to high school, but would encourage them to pursue their interests so that they succeed.

### Desire for Power and Control

All people like power and to control other people. There is nothing wrong about that because it is a natural tendency. However, that hunger for power and the desire to control others become problematic if they are pursued without considering how such pursuits may make other people feel. Most societies expect the husband to have power over the wife and to be able to control her. Among the Shona, sometimes men are advised to give their newlyweds a thorough thrashing for no apparent reason except to prove that they are in charge. There are many cases where a woman feels entitled to wield the power and control in the home, but the man has to wrestle that power from the woman through battering, isolating, neglecting or insulting the wife. The abuse increases if the wife tries to resist the control of the husband.

In the Shona culture, a wife belongs to the whole extended family. Although her husband enjoys the exclusive rights over her with regards to sex, other family members have their rights too. For instance, they can send the woman to do domestic chores for them and she is bound to comply even if she does not want to. If the woman refuses to do that, it can be reported to the husband who is expected to show his power and control over the wife in one way or the other. Men who do not listen to complaints from their family members might be accused of being under *petticoat government* that refers to a situation where the woman has power and control over the husband. Sometimes such men are charged with being under the influence of a love potion. One of the reason, Shona people encourage men to marry younger women is an attempt to create a situation where the older husband can overpower and control the younger woman. A younger woman would look up to the older husband for both sustenance and wisdom. In the case of a physical confrontation between the two, a younger woman would be easier to subdue and subjugate than a female who is older than the husband.

## Cultural Practices

Cultural practices have been fingered by many domestic violence activists as a causal factor of domestic violence. The United Nations encouraged concerned institutions and persons to investigate such cultural causes of domestic violence.[13] Among the Shona, the demand for privatized, commercialized, and exorbitant bridewealth is one of the causal factors of the violence against women. Chapter 3 of this book will explore how bridewealth contributes to violence against Shona women in Zimbabwe.

Besides that, it is a cultural expectation that men be more aggressive than females. This mentality has its origins in the dangers that were found in the primitive society. Men had to learn to be aggressive to protect their families from wild animals and other aggressors. Suman Kakar is of the opinion that, "in many societies, women grow up expecting men to be aggressive. In fact, many women expect their partners to use violence once in a while."[14] That is why people cry foul if a man is overpowered by his wife and becomes the subject of abuse—it is not normative. Among the Shona, the demand for privatized, commercialized, and exorbitant bridewealth is one of the causal factors of the violence against women.

Different cultural groups have different cultural practices that may be seen as abusive to women. Some cultures encourage men to marry younger women for easy control. Other cultures promote the educating of male children at the expense of girls. Some cultures allow men to discipline their wives by moderate beating. Some cultures allow men to have extra-marital affairs without being held accountable for their infidelity. Some cultures prevent women from running away from abusive marriages. There are also cultures that prevent women from reporting their abusive husbands to the law enforcement agents.

## Female Dependence

In pre-colonial Zimbabwe, women were expected to stay at home taking care of the kids and doing farming while men would be hunting, gathering, and fighting enemies. The woman's place was in the home. When the

13. United Nations, *Violence against Women*, 31, 37.
14. Kakar, *Domestic Abuse, Public Policy / Criminal Justice*, 191.

British arrived in 1890 and established mines, farms, and industries, most men started pursuing gainful employment in those industries. When men left their rural homes in search of jobs, they left their wives and children in their rural homes too. Those women were prevented from acquiring a new worldview from the White settlers. But, men learned new skills and a new language.

When the British type of education was introduced, most families preferred sending boys to school than girls. The preference for educating boys was influenced by both economic and cultural reasons. Among the Shona, every boy is expected to take care of his parents and siblings. Therefore, an educated boy would get a better job and would bring more wealth into the family. A Shona girl is different; she gets married, and if the husband pays bridewealth for her, he acquires her productive capacity. That is considered a waste by some people. Consequently, most Shona people would rather educate a boy child than a girl. The educated boys then joined the industries, commercial farms, and mines, and by so doing leaving the girls in the rural home helping the mother to do domestic chores. However, the preference of educating the boy child at the expense of the girl was not to remain forever. Eventually, more women started attaining the British type of education. They too got gainful employment in areas that originally were predominantly male. But, most women had already been left behind by men in terms of the acquisition of economic freedom, so, they continue to trail men in that respect.

Unequal educational opportunities between Shona boys and girls forced Shona women to depend on their husbands for livelihood. What Elizabeth Schneider said about the battered American woman is equally accurate about the urban battered Shona woman. She writes: "Many women who are battered have little money, no child care, no employment; they may financially and emotionally depend on the men who batter them; they believe that it is batter to stay with the men because of their children; or they don't want to leave because they love the men and want to maintain whatever intimacy and sense of connection they can."[15]

Abusive men take advantage of the financial situation of their loved ones. They know that such women have nowhere to go because they do not have the money to support themselves and the children if they dare. Although financial independence does not guarantee a Shona woman freedom from domestic violence, at least, such women have more economic freedom. Women with self-financial generating jobs or employment are likely to have higher self-esteem than women who are not gainfully employed. They are

15. Schneider, *Battered Women and Feminist Lawmaking*, 77.

not *broilers* or *home defenders*.[16] They contribute money for the upkeep of the family. Those women who do not bring money into the family are likely to feel demeaned and as a consequence, they might have low self-esteem. Financially stable women may decide to leave the abusive husband and still can make it in life, unlike the unemployed women.

## Alcohol and Drugs

Some men abuse their spouses when they are under the influence of alcohol. I had a cousin who would batter his wife whenever he had taken alcohol. Whenever there was a beer party, his wife expected to be beaten up. It is hard to know whether such spouse abusers do it because of the influence of alcohol or because they use alcohol as a scapegoat to abuse their partners. In the rural areas, some abusive men threaten their spouses by telling them that they would deal with them after taking alcohol.

Alcohol and drugs can be blamed for some of the violent behavior of men because of some observations. First, alcohol and drugs have an adverse influence on some takers. It seems that they make some men lose their cool and become argumentative and aggressive. Some men fight other men at the beer halls, but, others come home and beat up their wives. Second, alcohol and drugs take away the shame of abusing one's wife. Abusing one's partner is not only embarrassing to the victim, but also to the abuser. That is why every abuser tries to justify his actions. Third, alcohol and drugs give some men the courage to engage in violent acts that they would not have the courage to do when sober. Finally, some men use alcohol and drugs as scapegoats so that they can always say, "I did that because I was drunk." Such men try to convince their spouses that alcohol is the problem, not themselves. Some victims argue that their abusive husbands are good, but, alcohol is bad.

## Jealousy and Possessiveness

According to Lenore E. Walker, jealousy is almost universally present in battering relationships.[17] Both men and women in relationships can be very jealous and possessive of the other. Whether jealous comes from the hus-

16. *Broilers* are hybrid chickens that are known for their insatiable appetite. The term is used derogatively to refer to unemployed wives who stay at home expecting husbands to support them. *Home defender* is another derogative term for women who are not gainfully employed and stay at home as if their main responsibility was to guard the home and household properties from being stolen by thieves.

17. Walker, *The Battered Woman*, 114.

band or the wife the consequences are almost similar. Jealousy, in its right proportion, shows that the spouses love each other. But, if excessively done, it damages trust in a relationship. A wife who is too possessive of the husband is likely to be upset whenever the husband comes home late or speaks with other women. Possessiveness may lead to unnecessary quarrels, and those quarrels may degenerate into physical violence.

If a husband is too possessive, he may begin to treat his wife as his personal property. She is not allowed to talk to other men even at the workplace. She may not be permitted to associate with other women because these are accused of influencing her negatively. Jealousy and possessiveness lead to the isolation of the victim. She is brainwashed into thinking that she is not capable of making her own decisions. I knew of men who would beat up their wives if they come back from work and find the shoe prints of a man passing through their premises. Some women would sweep the threshold whenever a man passes through their homestead to erase the boot prints. In the mind of a possessive man, he sees treachery and unfaithfulness in every move that his wife makes. Sometimes, the husband chooses what the woman should wear when she is going out. Some women are not allowed to go out shopping alone. Possessiveness in relationships imprisons, isolates, demeans, and dehumanizes, the beloved. Love that hurts the beloved is not love at all. It sows the seeds of resentment and hatred. Love should set the beloved free rather than enslaving her.

### Extra-marital Affairs

In Zimbabwe, extra-marital affairs of the husband cause a lot of pain to the lawful wife, but at times, there is nothing she can do to stop it. If a husband is involved in extramarital affairs, he may begin to ill-treat his wife. The ill-treatment might take several different forms. He may neglect his wife emotionally, financially, and conjugally. Some men may refuse to eat their wives' food or to share bedrooms with them. In most cases, such neglect may force the woman to complain, and the husband may punish her for such complaints. There are instances where the lawful wife attacks her husband's mistress, and that may lead to the abuse of the wife by the husband in support of his mistress.

If a married woman is apprehended having an extra-marital affair, it can lead to divorce or the severe disciplining of the wife by the husband. In the Shona culture, married women and men are expected to be faithful to each other. However, unfaithful men can get away with it, most of the times, but women get punished in one way or the other. Traditionally, it was not recommended to divorce a cheating woman but to shame her. Her illicit lover, if apprehended by the husband or revealed by the wife under interrogation during childbirth, was required to pay compensation to the husband. This revelation was known as *kudura*. The compensation was usually in the form of cows of which one was slaughtered. Some meat portion of the slaughtered cow was roasted and consumed by the illicit lover and formal husband as a sign of reconciliation. The major setback of receiving compensation for the adulterous woman was that the husband would not have trust in the wife, and it was likely that the illicit affair would continue. The shame and embarrassment such a publication of the forbidden affair lowered the self-esteem of the woman, not of the man who in some circles was considered a *hero*. She became the laughing stock of the village because she was considered a prostitute. Her children and relatives would be embarrassed by her infidelity as well.

## Types of Domestic Violence

### *Wife battering*

Wife battering is the most distinct type of domestic violence among the Shona because it is physical and outsiders can detect its occurrence. Although both abusers and victims may try to conceal its existence, they are sometimes not successful because of the noises, shouting, and cries that both the perpetrator and victim produce. Sometimes victims sustain injuries that may need medical attention, and at most medical facilities victims are required to tell the truth about the cause of their injuries so that they can receive medical treatment.

Battering is also the most dangerous form of domestic violence because it may cause severe injuries or even the death of the victim. Some people think that wife beating does not become wife battering unless it is often repeated. Lenore E. Walker describes a battered woman as "a woman who is repeatedly subjected to any forceful physical or psychological behavior by a man to coerce her to do something he wants her to do without any concern for her rights."[18] However, other anti-domestic violence activists have argued that any form of wife beating; even a single slap may also be referred to as wife battering and the survivor, a battered woman. They think that trivialization of some types of beating may lead some women to believe that slapping or shoving is not a serious offense and as such should not be reported. Leddy lists various types of battering that victims may have

18. Ibid., xv.

to endure such as shooting, stabbing, choking, burning, shoving, kicking, pushing, slapping, stalking, chasing, biting, and spitting.[19]

How many Zimbabwean women are victims and survivors of wife battering? Since domestic violence is a silent crime, many researchers agree that getting accurate statistics on it is extremely hard. Victims may not be willing to reveal the brutalities that their loved ones subject them to. Miranda Davies supports the above notion when she says that domestic violence is a hidden problem and as a result, it is difficult to come up with exact statistics about the crime.[20] According to her, there are many reasons for the lack of statistics. She writes: "Victims are often reluctant to report because they feel ashamed of being assaulted by their husbands; they may be afraid; they may have a sense of loyalty. The actual extent of violence in the home may never be accurately known but it is clear that such violence is part of the dynamics of many family situations in both the developed and developing world."[21]

A report produced by Musasa Project in 1998 stated that 42% of the women in the Midlands Province of Zimbabwe had experienced physical violence, such as slaps, beatings, choking, and, others.[22] In its pamphlet titled *Domestic Violence (Prevention and Protection of the Victims) Bill* 2003, Musasa Project states that:

> Domestic violence is a substantial problem in Zimbabwe. On average every woman in Zimbabwe will suffer some form of domestic violence during her lifetime. A study conducted by Musasa Project in 1996 showed that domestic violence in Zimbabwe is very rampant. The results of this study showed the following: 1 in 4 women has been physically abused, i.e. kicked hit, or beaten. 1 in 4 women had been forced to have sex by their partners. 1 in 6 women were prevented from seeing relatives. 1 in 6 women were prevented from getting a job or going to work.[23]

In another study that Musasa Project carried out in 2000, domestic violence was among the leading causes of death for women in the 15 to 40 age group in Zimbabwe.[24] In 2006, the same Project recorded 4,413 new clients and 3,084 of the clients had problems related to physical and or psychological abuse.[25] Apart from the studies that have been done by Musasa

19. Ibid., 20.

20. Davies, *Women and Violence*, 2.

21. Ibid., 4.

22. Musasa Project, *Regional Skills Clinic*.

23. Musasa Project, *Domestic Violence (Prevention and Protection of Victims) Bill*.

24. Ibid.

25. Ibid.

Project, there are the daily stories recorded in Zimbabwe's daily newspapers like the Herald concerning domestic violence. Cases of either women or husbands axing their spouses to death have been reported.[26]

## Forced Sex

Of all the abuses that victims of domestic violence can suffer, marital rape is the most secretive. In Zimbabwe, just like in most countries, sex is sacred, and people do not perform it or talk about it openly. Forced sex happens when the husband engages in sex with his wife without her verbal or symbolic consent and readiness. The concept of marital rape is very strange to the Shona. The primary challenge that Shona victims encounter in this respect is that men pay for exclusive sexual rights over their wives. The Shona man thinks that it is his right to have sex with his wife whenever he wants it, and in any manner that he deems appropriate because he has paid for that. The part of the bridewealth that deals with that is *rugaba* or *rutsambo*. It would be considered absurd for a Shona woman to report the marital rape to anyone because everyone knows that the husband would have paid bridewealth so that he can acquire and enjoy that right. Even the parents of the victimized woman would be very much embarrassed and scandalized to learn that their daughter would have reported her husband for raping her. In fact, such allegations would embarrass not only the parents of the victim but also other members of the community.

The lack of witnesses is another setback to victims. Marital rape happens behind bolted doors. Even in circumstances where there is evidence of sexual activity between the husband and wife on the day in question, it may be hard for the law enforcement agents to determine if the man would have compelled his wife to have sex with him. It would be the word of the woman against that of the husband.

The other challenge that Shona women encounter with regards to marital rape is that of infidelity. A man who is frequently denied his conjugal rights might get involved with other women with the blessings of his relatives. The surest way for a woman to chase away her husband to other women is to deny him sex. Besides that, such women are suspected of getting sexual gratification from other men clandestinely. So, for a Shona woman to keep her man away from extra-marital affairs or even taking a second wife, she has to comply with his conjugal demands, even if they are unreasonable and insatiable. Consequently, marital rape remains a silent scourge in many cultures.

26. *The Zimbabwe Herald* of August 28, 2007 reported of a Beitbridge man who fatally axed his sixteen-year-old wife.

*Denial of Financial Support*

Denial of financial support is usually made to unemployed women who solely depend on their husbands for daily sustenance. Often, such men squander their salaries with other women or in beer drinking. Some of those men do not come back home on pay days until all the money is gone. When they finally return, they expect the wife to serve them food that they know is not available. They want the wife to wash their clothes, yet they know that there is no washing detergent. In the rural areas, such women do menial jobs in other people's fields to get food for the family.

Denial of financial support is usually tinged with battering. The husband comes home empty-handed. The wife demands some money to buy food. The man gets angry and batters the woman. Sometimes the battering happens before the woman says anything. It is intended to silence the woman. In some cases, if the woman gets into vegetable marketing, the husband may demand the money that comes from the wife's sales of vegetable. The main challenge for such women is not knowing where one's next meal will come from and the perpetual struggle to pay school fees for the children.

*Psychological Abuse*

Psychological abuse takes several forms, and its purpose is to lower the self-esteem of the victim. The husband may deny the wife access to her clothes. In one of the many abusive incidents between my mother and father, I remember my father shouting that he wanted my mother to give him all her clothes because he had bought them for her. I do not remember the details of the demands, but I know that they had something to do with the clothes. I remember my brother saying that, "mama, why don't you give him the clothes so that he stops beating you?" My brother was severely punished by my father for saying that. Some men may force their wives to wear some particular clothes that the men deem appropriate. I think that it is good for either spouse to recommend particular clothes for each other, but, it should be left to the spouse receiving advice to decide. Among the Shona, the husband may forbid his wife to wear trousers, mini-skirts, and other types of clothes even if that is what the woman wants to wear. That belittles the woman as someone who cannot choose what to wear.

Sometimes the man may deny his wife conjugal rights. The husband might do that as a form of disciplining the wife or to show her that she is dispensable and no longer loved. If the woman demands her conjugal rights openly, the husband may beat her up or insult her. Such insulting might be done in the presence of neighbors and her children to shame the wife and lower her self-esteem.

The husband may beat up the wife in the presence of her friends so that they laugh at her. Sometimes the man tells other people of his wife's secrets. Some men accuse their wives of infidelity in the presence of other persons so that they can be viewed as prostitutes. Other men accuse their wives of being witches; people who possess mysterious powers to harm others secretly so that they may devour their flesh. That accusation diminishes the self-esteem of the accused woman. The man can go ahead and abuse the woman without anyone coming to her aid because she is a witch. Although some people who are accused of being witches might be real witches, many are charged with being witches just to dehumanize them.

## Verbal Attacks

There are domestic violence victims who argue that verbal attacks are more painful and long-lasting than physical assault. They are intended to completely dehumanize and destroy the opponent. Men who do that take advantage of the trust that is found in marriages. They use whatever information that they know about their wives to humiliate them. An abusive man can insult the wife's mother and father, in the process. Verbal attacks are more painful because they reflect the truth about the victim that could have been shared in trust and intimacy. Some of the insults may look this, "You are a prostitute just like your mother. You are a witch like your mom. You are as dirty and lazy just like your mom. Your father is a thief." Sometimes the insults take a sexual flavor, "You are not good in bed. You are not as sweet in bed as other women."

If the insulted woman tries to retaliate, she may be overpowered and then subjected to a physical assault. Suppose the aggrieved woman responds as follows: "How about you? Do you think that you are a real man? There are better men than you. You are pathetic in bed." Among the Shona, such an insult might not be forgiven. Such a woman might be accused of infidelity and may be divorced. She would be queried on how she knows about other men's sexual performances if she has not slept with them. Moreover, every Shona man gets hurt if his sexual prowess is questioned, particularly by his wife. So, the same insults that can be used for women might not be used for men without devastating results for the woman who uses them for her husband.

## Denial of Conjugal Rights

Sexual intercourse is at the center of almost every marriage. Of course, other benefits such as children are also important, but sex remains pivotal in all sexual relationships. If the wife is denied financial support, she can get it from relatives or other well-wishers, but if she is denied sex she may not get it from elsewhere. In some cases, men who refuse their wives conjugal rights do have affairs elsewhere, but some men just do that to humiliate the woman. Sometimes it is done to force the woman into submission.

The other form of the denial of conjugal rights concerns a sexual encounter between husband and wife that are not satisfying to the woman. The husband does not care whether his wife derives as much pleasure as he does in the sexual act. There is no foreplay, and he does not wait for the wife to reach orgasm. In fact, the abuser does not care whether his partner enjoys sex or not, he just wants to please himself. Such sex is as bad as having no sex at all. It is a cruel denial of the sexual fulfillment by the man that every married woman deserves. The man would be using the woman as a sex object. It is a fact that some men fail to satisfy their wives sexually not by design but because of the lack of skills of how to do that. But, whether the failure is by design or accident, it is a misuse of one's manhood, and an abuse of the woman's sexuality, and consequently, a shameful form of domestic violence.

## Inciting the Children

Every parent would like to be loved by her or his children. Among the Shona, swaying the love of the children from the father is a common thing in domestic politics because the mother spends more time with the children. But, some men turn their children against the mother by claiming to be the victim. Such a man may accuse the woman of overspending money on trivialities although the husband would have given the woman inadequate funds. Sometimes wives are accused of infidelity in the presence of children so that they lose their children's trust and respect. Sometimes the children stick by their mother's side despite the demonization that the father does to her. However, more often than not, children may be brainwashed into hating their mother. Some men buy the loyalty of the children with gifts and money. To be rejected by one's husband might be far much better than to be hated by one's children.

## Isolation

The isolation of the woman is intended to prevent her from getting help from anybody. Such women might not be permitted to visit their relatives. They may not be authorized to have friends. They may not go shopping alone. They may not be allowed to attend church and other social gatherings. They may not be permitted to open a social media accounts such as Facebook or Twitter. The husband may check the wife's cell phone for calls and messages that come through from people he does not know. Sometimes victims are prevented from getting any employment that will take them outside the home and would give them some freedom. The purpose of isolating the wife is to control, exploit, subjugate, dehumanize, demean, and frighten her. It is also intended to put the woman in her place of servitude. Since the abuser should be her only friend, she should see and interpret reality, according to the lenses of her abuser.

## Making Major Decisions Alone

Some husbands can be abusive by making major decisions that affect the family without consulting their wives. A man might take all the money that his wife earns so that the wife will have to beg him for money whenever she needs to buy something. At times there are threats and coercion.[27] When the two go shopping for furniture and other household property, the husband does all the choosing. He may choose the dresses that the wife should buy. Some men may give money to their relatives without the consent of the woman. They may resign from their jobs without agreeing with the woman. Some may decide to sell their houses or cars without consulting the women. Some men give away their clothes to friends or relatives without the knowledge of the wives. Among the Shona, some men completely ignore women during bridewealth negotiations. In families where women are invited to participate in the negotiations, the paternal aunt may have more authority that the mother of the bride. Although the mother of the bride is allowed to decide about some of the small portions of the bridewealth that fall under her jurisdiction, the amount of the major portions is almost always determined by the men.

27. Leddy, "Domestic Violence," 18.

*Comments*

Usually, the above abuses are not suffered in isolation because one victim may be subjected to one or more of the abuses. Some perpetrators of violence may use wife battering as the last resort, to compel the woman to accept other violent acts silently. Some abusers never graduate to the physical beating of the wives. All the types of domestic violence are done to dehumanize, embarrass, subjugate, and oppress the victim.

## Why do Battered Women Stay

All forms of secret domestic violence come into the open at one point during their occurrence. The question that most anti-domestic violence activists, relatives, and friends of the victimized woman ask is, "why does the abused woman stay?" Although this question is relevant, it is not useful because it implies that the victim has the power to leave the abuser, and since she does not leave, she is equally blameworthy of the abuses that she experiences. Most anti-domestic violence activists think that this question further victimizes the victim because domestic violence does worse to the victim than what the eye can see, and the ear can hear. Several reasons have been given as to why the abused woman continues to stay with the abuser.

*Economic Dependence*

Many abused women stay with their abusers because they know that they cannot make it financially by themselves. As explained earlier, in Zimbabwe, fewer women have well-paying jobs if they do have jobs at all. Traditionally, the woman's place was the home where she did all domestic work; cooking, looking after the kids, washing clothes, and working in the fields. Although the independent government of Zimbabwe tried all that it could to emancipate women in all spheres of life, most women are still lagging behind their male counterparts, economically. Some abused women know very well that they depend financially on the abusers, and life would be tough if they decide to leave. In some cases, divorced men have been asked by the courts to support the divorced women and children who are under the age of eighteen. However, men have devised ways of running away from that responsibility without inviting the full wrath of the law.

## Children

Some women stay with their abusers because they do not want to leave their children with the abuser. Traditionally, children of the Shona couples belong to the husband because a portion of the bridewealth would have given them absolute rights over the children. In the past, if there were any divorce, the children would remain with the father, but young kids would go with the mother, with the full knowledge that they still belonged to their father. Now, with the coming of new marriage laws, although the wife can win the custody of children, customarily, they are supposed to belong to their father. Sometimes, divorced men marry again, and it is believed that stepmothers do not take proper care of another woman's children. So, some abused women may decide to stay so that they can take care of their children.

## Bridewealth

Although the practice of bridewealth will be discussed in detail in chapter 3, it suffices to say a few things about it here. Bridewealth is refundable, so, customarily the parents of any woman who divorces her husband may be asked to refund some of the bridewealth that was paid for her. In most cases, the bridewealth would have been already spent, and it would be hard for the parents of the abused woman to refund it. That is the reason some parents would encourage their abused daughters to stick with their abusers.

Bridewealth also empowers abusive husbands to pursue their runaway wives and to negotiate their coming back to their marital homes. It also gives the man exclusive sexual rights over the woman, so, the talk of marital rape may draw scorn upon the victimized woman. It also empowers the husband to discipline the wife by moderate beating and gives him rights over her productive capacity. Most Shona women believe that all marriages are not smooth, and sacrifices have to be made. So, they stay.

## Religious Beliefs

Some religions teach that women should be submissive to their husbands in all things without giving exceptions. That message is repeated many times until some women fanatically believe it. To worsen the matter, some religions make it very difficult for women to divorce their husbands legally. Those women who go ahead and divorce their husbands may find it hard to be accepted by their religious groups. Some divorced women become ostracized from their religious communities and might not be permitted to partake in the sacred rituals of their religious communities. That further victimization may force the abused woman to stay with her violent husband. If she decides to leave her abusive husband, she receives no sympathy from her parents, culture, and church. For some women, leaving the abuser might result in more abuses than if they had remained with their single abusers.

## Self-Blame

Some abusive men know the art of apportioning blame upon the victim. They know how to convince the victim that her own shortcomings cause the abuse. The abused woman begins to believe that she is battered because she cannot cook properly or that she is not a good lady. Since she believes that she is an evil person, running away will not solve the problem because she will continue to be herself. If she were to remarry, she believes that the same issues would follow her. It is true that sometimes the woman makes some mistakes, but to accept abuse as a way of expiating one's imperfections might not be acceptable. Both the man and the woman make mistakes, but to think that only women should be disciplined by beating is to demean women. Self-blame also instills embarrassment in the victim.

## Love for the Abuser

Some abused women love their abusers. They remain with them because of love. To persuade them to leave their abusers is like trying to influence them to divorce their husbands. Such victims may accuse their female friends, who give them the advice to run away and seek assistance, of jealousy. "They want me to divorce my husband because they also love him. They are jealous of my good life." Moreover, some violent men claim to love their wives. Some of those men know how to convince the victims that they love them. Communities are full of women who would be spoiled with gifts by their husbands after every battering episode. The battering is covered up by the gifts.

In fact, some women believe that the fact that they are battered does not give evidence that their husbands do not love them. Sometimes, relatives are successful in persuading the abused woman to run away and seek help, but in some cases, those parents become enemies when the wife and husband reconcile, as they sometimes do. Because of that, some relative choose to leave alone the couple that is involved in an abusive relationship.

## Fear

Fear is multi-faceted and the greatest impediment to making new decisions. In a violent marriage, there is fear of the abuser himself. The victim believes that if she runs away, the abuser would be able to track her down and that might worsen the situation when she is brought back home. There is also a fear of leaving the children with the violent father. There is fear that the abuser might turn the children against her. There is fear of the unknown if a divorce happens. There is fear of economic hardships that wait in the future. There is fear of the failure to get another husband, and of being blamed for the breakup of the marriage. There is fear of being demonized by one's relatives, religious community, and friends. There is fear of becoming the laughing stock of the society. There is fear of the change of the marital status from being married to single. Those concerns force some abused women to continue hoping that the perpetrator would change. So, they stay.

## Low Self-esteem

Low self-esteem is the feeling that one is unworthy, and consequently, one does not deserve the respect, dignity, and value that are awarded other people. Women who experience low self-esteem think that they are not equal to other women who are not abused by their husbands. They do not value themselves, and they do not have confidence in what they can do. In Zimbabwe, low self-esteem can be caused by many issues. First, Shona women are expected to remain virgins until marriage, but, sometimes that does not happen. Knowing what their husbands expect from them women who would have lost their virginity before marriage might feel guilty. Sometimes men do not ask their newlyweds about how they would have lost their virginity, but that silence might not mean that the husband does not nurse such questions. Sometimes abusive men remind their wives of the absence of virginity at wedding later in marriage.

Second, low self-esteem can be the result of the woman being not as educated as the husband. Some of those husbands would then belittle their wives or even force them to go back to school. Those women who would continuously fail to pass their qualifying examinations will feel guilty. Lack of education is connected to the women being unemployed.

Third, some women have convinced themselves that they are ugly, and, therefore, do not deserve their handsome husbands. They think that the husbands are doing them a favor by abusing them and not divorcing them. They think that they may never be able to land another man if they lose the one that they do have.[28]

## Comments

Domestic violence is social cancer that is difficult to cure. Although the government of Zimbabwe has done many things to emancipate Zimbabwean women from oppressive patriarchal structures, a lot still needs to be done. The United Nations states that domestic violence happens within the settings of male dominance; "These include: exploitation of women's productive and reproductive work; control over women's sexuality and reproductive capacity; cultural norms and practices that entrench women's unequal status . . ."[29] In Zimbabwe, what the United Nations says is epitomized in the religious and cultural practice of bridewealth. Chapter 3 will argue that as long as bridewealth remains commercialized in Zimbabwe, the total emancipation of the Zimbabwean women will remain utopian because its payment or promise to pay it, gives husbands particular rights that women do not gain in the same transaction.

28. For a more detailed explanation why abused women stay in other cultural set-ups, consult Kakar, *Domestic Abuse, Public Policy / Criminal Justice.*

29. United Nations, *Violence against Women*, 29.

# Chapter 2

## Types of Shona Marriages

MARRIAGE IS ONE OF the inalienable and natural rights that most free human beings have enjoyed since time immemorial. Every human society assures its people of that fundamental and natural imperative to marry and procreate. Some religions claim that the right to marry was instituted by God or some other divinities for the purpose of procreation and companionship. Hence, most religions have laid down rules that ensure the smooth, faithful, and orderly practice of marriage. Every free man and woman, in every society, irrespective of his or her color, race, economic status, the level of education, and political affiliation is guaranteed the right to marry, at least one woman or man.

In Africa, marriage is a religious obligation that all people who are able should embrace.[1] Yates Jr. explains why marriage is a religious commitment in Africa. He observes that "Marriage brings together man and woman, families, clans, and also the ancestors and the unborn since it is through the past and the future that the group's identity is remembered and sustained."[2] He goes on to say that in African societies, a person who is not married is "generally considered abnormal and unfulfilled."[3] So, a deliberate decision not to marry is not only an insult to oneself and one's family members but, also to the bigger community and ancestors. It is considered a deliberate rejection to perpetuate the human race.

People approach marriage in a manner that is different from how most animals approach the same phenomenon. In the animal kingdom, the most

1. Mbiti, *African Religions and Philosophy*, 1.
2. Yates Jr., "African Traditional Religion," 43.
3. Ibid., 43.

potent male may enjoy the monopoly of sexual intimacy with whichever female he may want, usually at the exclusion and deprivation of weaker males. The human society is different. It is orderly. There are laws that regulate marriages in all societies. The marriage regulations were perhaps, put in place by leaders to ensure that no person was deprived of the right to marry by selfish and powerful individuals, and also to prevent people from abusing the institution of marriage. The Shona people of Zimbabwe put in place many types of marriages to ensure that anybody who wanted to marry would have an opportunity to do so. This chapter explores the Shona types of marriage some of which are no longer in use.

## Kukumbira

*Kukumbira* is the conventional form of marriage among the Shona of Zimbabwe. A man identifies a woman that he loves and the two fall in love. Traditionally, it was the responsibility of the man to ask a woman out. However, if a female loved an unaware man, she had other ways of making her feelings known to the man, but she was not expected to take the initiative to propose love to him. Even after the man proposed love to her finally, she was not supposed to accept the long-awaited proposal, at once. She had to beat about the bush at first, and then accept the proposal, eventually. That was a sign of a morally upright woman. Now, things have changed. Some daring women can take the initiative to propose love to men, and the Shona society is beginning to accept that.

There were some young men who were too shy to propose love to the girls that they loved. Such young men were assisted by friends or their aunts to make sure that the girl that they loved secretly became aware of their intentions and feelings. The person who assisted someone to propose love to a girl was known as *gwevedzi,* meaning the one who draws two people together. The same was done for girls who found it hard to attract a suitable marriage partner. Someone had to connect them to a young man who was interested. There was no payment given to the *gwevedzi* for his or her services. It was everyone's business to assist those people who were eligible to find a marriage partner.

A couple of weeks after a man and woman fell in love, they were expected to exchange love tokens known as *nduma,* which in most cases were handkerchiefs. There were instances where girls exchanged their dresses for a shirt as love tokens, but that was rare since dresses and shirts were expensive. Although there were no vows exchanged during the transaction, the love tokens were a sign that the two persons involved, loved each other seriously and wished to take their relationship to the next level, which was marriage. In the event of a breakup of the relationship, both parties were supposed to return the love token to its owner. Nowadays the love token has been replaced by the engagement ring although some lovers still exchange gifts.

The two lovers are supposed to abstain from premarital sexual activities because that can lead to unplanned pregnancies and was considered immoral. Negotiating bridewealth for a noticeably pregnant woman lowers the bargaining power of the woman's relatives. It is assumed that if the woman is not pregnant at the time of the bridewealth negotiations, then, there were no pre-marital sexual activities between the two. When the time to start marriage negotiations comes, the would-be son-in-law (*mukwasha*) sends his emissary known as *munyayi* or *dombo* to the family of the girl to initiate the negotiations. The *munyayi*, together with the relatives of the woman sets up a date on which the marriage negotiations would begin. Of course, the commencement of the marriage negotiations does not authorize the woman to start living with her husband as his wife. Consequently, the woman does not join her husband's family until all the negotiations are finalized and a considerable amount of bridewealth has been paid. Some Christian parents demand that a Christian wedding be conducted first before the woman is authorized to live with her husband. The major components of bridewealth will be discussed in chapter 3.

Most Shona people think that *Kukumbira* is the ideal type of marriage because it gives assurance that once the negotiations have started, the process will reach its logical conclusion—a wedding. The fact that the man, without duress, comes to seek the woman's hand in marriage makes her relatives proud and dignified. Munyaradzi Mawere and Annastincia Mbindi Mawere describe *kukumbira* as "the most legitimate and esteemed traditional customary marriage system."[4] It is believed to give value to the woman because she can be given away in marriage after a substantial amount of bridewealth would have been paid. It also shows that the girl would have managed to discipline herself regarding sexual desires since she is presumed to be a virgin at this point, unless if she is a single mother.

Although there are many advantages of the *kukumbira* type of marriage, especially for the woman and her relatives, it is mostly for those young men who can pay a substantial part of the bridewealth before they can take the bride to their homes. For poor men, the search for bridewealth may delay or put off the wedding indefinitely. Resultantly, they might opt for other forms of marriage. *Kukumbira* can also be abused by the parents of the

4. Mawere and Mawere, "The Changing Philosophy of African Marriage," 226.

woman because they can use her as leverage in their bridewealth negotiations. Since the woman is still in her parents' home and she is presumed to be a virgin, so, the would-be husband has to pay the requested bridewealth or ship out.

## Kutema Ugariri (Labor Marriage)

This type of marriage is no longer in effect nowadays. It was a form of marriage that was designed to ensure that men from underprivileged families who could not afford to pay bridewealth could still get wives. The period of labor provision would differ from family to family. Usually, it was around ten years. *Ugariri* can be divided into three basic categories. All the three types involved the labor provider's identification of a family that would accept labor bridewealth because not all parents accepted it. The first group included a man who would negotiate with his future father-in-law that he intended to provide labor as a form of bridewealth for his daughter who was yet to be born. If the father-in-law agreed, the man would start working for him even before the father-in-law bears a girl child.[5] Eventually, a girl would be born, and when she reached puberty, the father-in-law or his successor would permit the two to marry. Patience and the ability to work were two of the most desirable virtues for labor bridewealth.

The second category involved a man who would provide labor services for a young girl who is not yet old enough to marry. In such cases, depending on the age of the girl, the man would not wait too long before the woman reached puberty. If, by that time, the labor that the son-in-law would have rendered is adequate, then, the father of the woman would authorize the two to marry. There were instances where the man and the woman would be permitted to marry even before the man completed the agreed number of years in which he had to provide labor. That was based on the trust that the family had on the labor provider. The understanding was that the son-in-law and his wife would continue to render their labor to the family of the woman until the agreed number of years were completed.

The third category involved a man that was in love with a particular woman and intended to marry her. Both the man and the woman would realize that their intention to marry would not be successful because of the lack of bridewealth. So, the man would propose to use his labor as a form of bridewealth. If his request were granted, then he would begin to work for his prospective father-in-law without getting any salary, for an agreed number of years. Most of the times, the young man would be allowed to

---

5. Chigwedere, *Lobola*, 27.

stay with his fiancée's people but without engaging in sexual activities with the woman until his labor earned him the trust of her relatives. However, some families would immediately allow the son-in-law to begin to live with their daughter as husband and wife, as long as they promised that the man would continue to render his labor to the family of the woman. The couple could build their temporary home on the land that belonged to the father-in-law so that the man's labor services could be accessed quickly. If the man decided to run away from his wife and father-in-law before he completed the agreed years of labor provision, the father-in-law had the rights over the children and could get the outstanding bridewealth when one of the female children married.

This type of marriage shows how the marital needs of all Shona men were respected and fulfilled, even if they could not pay bridewealth. Any Shona man could marry a woman even if he were poor. However, there was some stigma attached to this kind of marriage. It was a form of marriage for the poor. Some parents who expected to get bridewealth in the form of cows and money did not accept labor bridewealth. The service bridewealth was also unpopular because it would not bring immediate wealth to the woman's family. Material bridewealth was needed because some of it would be used to acquire wives for the brothers of the woman, and that would be impossible if labor were used as a form of bridewealth. Furthermore, there was too much waiting on the part of the son-in-law. In some cases, he waited for the birth of his would-be wife. He waited for the girl to grow up. He also waited for the father-in-law's permission for the two to marry. In cases, where the father-in-law failed to bear a baby girl then the labor would have been provided in vain.

The other demerit of this type of marriage was that the groom was vulnerable to abuse by the bride's family. The relatives of the would-be wife knew very well that the man relied on their kindness, integrity, and honest. There was always the fear that the father-in-law could change his mind. He also could ill-treat him so as to force him to quit before he could get the woman for whom he had been working. *Ugariri* also violated the right to free choice to the young girls who were involved. They had to comply with their parents' decisions. Finally, in most cases, there was a significant age difference between the spouses, and consequently, some young girls would resent marrying an older man.

Although most of those women could not run away from their older husbands, there was some probability of them engaging in extra-marital affairs with younger men. This type of marriage was abandoned because of the monetization of the economy of Zimbabwe and the establishment of industries and gainful employment by the British. The arrival of the British heralded a new economic and social order in which each man would find a job, earn some money, and then, pay his own bridewealth. Before the monetization of the economy and the establishment of industries in Zimbabwe, most young men relied on their parents or relatives for bridewealth.

## Musengabere (Kidnapping Marriages)

This type of marriage is no longer practiced by the Shona people. A young man, who would have proposed love to a particular girl in the community to no avail, could ambush that girl when she would be going to the well to fetch some water or to the bush to bring some firewood, and would kidnap her. In a surprise attack, the rejected lover would grab the girl by the hand and force march her to his parents' home. If the woman were unwilling to walk, the kidnapper would carry her on his shoulders all the way back to his home. *Musengabere* was done by men from wealthy families who could afford to pay a substantial amount of bridewealth and would get the approval of the father-in-law, to marry his daughter.

It should be noted that *musengabere* was performed on mature girls who were ready for marriage rather than little girls. In the traditional Shona society, this kidnaping was legal, and could lead to a happy and lifelong marriage between the kidnaped and the kidnaper. Once the kidnaped woman set her feet on the kidnaper's premises, then she could not run away because she was already someone's wife. Besides that, the kidnaper and his relatives had to guard the bride until marriage negotiations started after which it would be futile for the bride to try to escape. One of the primary strengths of this form of marriage was that even the most unlikable men could marry the women that they loved. *Musengabere* had disadvantages too, one of which was that it violated the rights of the captured woman by depriving her of choosing her future husband. Furthermore, *musengabere* was used as a desperate and last resort by a disillusioned and desperate man, and most Shona groups despised it. The above could be some of the reasons the Shona abandoned this form of marriage.

## Kuganha

Tabona Shoko is of the opinion that *kuganha* is the female equivalent of *musengabere*.[6] *Kuganha* literally means to impose oneself upon another, particularly for marriage purposes. It was done by a girl who would have loved someone for a long time, and would have tried to entice the man in

---

6. Shoko, *Karanga Indigenous Religion in Zimbabwe*, 27.

question, in many different ways, without succeeding to spring the man into initiating the courtship. Since it was taboo for a Shona woman to propose love to a boy first even if she loved him desperately, she had to wait for the man to take the initiative. Sometimes the wait was forever because some boys never paid attention to such willing girls. Be that as it may, the Shona culture provided a solution to that problem. The woman could just impose herself on the man that she loved.

The process was simple. The concerned woman would just pack her belongings and go to the home of one of the relatives of the man that she loved, and she would then demand the boy's hand in marriage. It worked out for some girls. According to Tabona Shoko, the man could not resist such a woman because a wife or husband is considered a gift from the ancestors, and what ancestors give should not be resisted.[7] Again, this type of marriage was not popular because it demeaned the girl, to some extent. Hence, very few girls would brave the winds by imposing themselves on unsuspecting men. Although Shona men were permitted to marry as many wives as they could afford, the *kuganhwa* husband was more likely to take a second wife to the chagrin of the senior wife. The other setback to *kuganha* was that the bargaining power of the woman's relatives would be reduced and consequently, little bridewealth would be paid for her. This form of marriage has since been abandoned by the Shona.

## Kutizisa (Elopement)

The *kutizisa* form of marriage demands that the involved man and woman have to be in love first. Usually, the man's family would not have the necessary bridewealth that is required to pursue a *kukumbira* form of marriage. Consequently, the two persons in love would arrange with the aunt of the woman so that the man's people would go and fetch her from her aunt's home. Small gifts would be given to the bride to encourage her to walk to her husband's home. As the party nears the home of the would-be husband, the woman is supposed to walk slowly and to ask for more money. If the man's relatives refuse to give her money or even to promise her that they would give her something when they reach home, the woman is expected to sit down and refuse to walk.

The mother of the eloped woman knows what would have happened to her daughter. At least, one day after the elopement, the mother should tell one of her husband's relatives that one of the daughters is missing. She has to pay a small fee to say that. As a result, no one worries about the missing

7. Ibid.

woman because they all know that she has eloped, and they look forward to the arrival of the husband's bridewealth negotiating team. After a few days, the family of the man sends an emissary to the relatives of the woman to begin the bridewealth negotiations. The only difference between *kutizisa* and *kukumbira* is that in the *kutizisa* form of marriage, the man and the woman start living together as husband and wife before the bridewealth negotiations begin, but, in *kukumbira*, negotiations precede living together of the two as husband and wife.

One of the fundamental advantages of this type of marriage is that there are no unnecessary delays in the living together of the woman and the man. It also reduces the bargaining capacity of the father-in-law to the advantage of the groom's relatives. If the father-in-law demands more bridewealth than the son-in-law is prepared to pay, the bridewealth negotiations may be delayed, but that does not stop the couple from living together as husband and wife. Of course, the father-in-law can remove his daughter from the man's home by force, and hold her until the man pays bridewealth to his satisfaction. This phenomenon is known as *kubatira pfuma*. Nowadays, many people see this removal of the daughter as a waste of effort because the woman can elope back to her husband or the husband may not follow-up the wife. This form of marriage is still alive among the Shona.

## Kutiza Mukumbo (Unplanned Pregnancy Marriages)

This type of marriage is also known as *kumitisa*, a word that was borrowed from the English word, *mating*. It happens when a woman who is in love with a particular man becomes pregnant before the marriage negotiations begin and the boy is not willing to do the *kutizisa*. In that case, the woman would pack her belongings and elope to her boyfriend's home. Some men may refuse to take responsibility for the pregnancy at first, but eventually, they do, after receiving counseling from their elders. If the man who is responsible for the pregnancy refuses to marry the woman, she will go back to her people who then, accompany her to her boyfriend's people to negotiate the payment of *damages*. The *damage* is a fee that a rejected woman's father charges to the man who is responsible for impregnating his daughter and then refuses to marry her. Some men accept the responsibility for the pregnancy but refuse to marry the woman. If the man who is responsible for the pregnancy confesses to having no love for the pregnant woman, all the negotiations would concern the payment of *damages*. Once the man pays the *damage*, the pregnant female can go back to her people. The child born out of that affair would later go to its father. Some men reject the responsibility for the pregnancy but accept the woman. When that happens, the woman can live with her husband if the two love each other, but, she should send her child to her parents or its biological father if known, after weaning.

One of the advantages that this type of marriage gives to the man is that he may choose not to marry the pregnant woman. Also, the rejected woman's relatives walk out of the negotiations with something for their daughter's loss of the *single* woman status. Yes, they may not receive bridewealth, but, they get the *damage* fees and at times their daughter's child.

One of the saddest disadvantages of this form of marriage is that the pregnant woman can be rejected by the man who is responsible for her pregnancy. Once a single woman gives birth to a baby it would be difficult for her to find another husband. Some Shona single mothers are lucky, they find husbands, but, some of those single mothers would suffer the separation from their children since they are not expected to bring them to their new husbands. Some of them would face the indignities of not fetching as much bridewealth as women who would not have born children before their marriages. Moreover, a pregnant woman who cannot find the responsible father of her unborn baby can be viewed as a projection of her mother's immorality. Consequently, some pregnant women who are no longer certain as to the identity of the father of the unborn baby may try several of their boyfriends if they have more than one until one of them accepts responsibility for the unborn child. But, if the involved men get to know about other boyfriends, they can use that as evidence of the pregnant girlfriend' sexual immorality and unfitness for marriage.

## Kuzvarira (Pledged Marriages)

This form of marriage can be compared to barter trade. It was initiated by the heads of impecunious families in times of desperation, particularly, starvation. The affected family would negotiate with some wealthy, elderly men for the exchange of grains or cows for a young girl for marriage. Usually, such men were old, and therefore, already married or widowed. If any of those men either wanted another wife or to replace a dead one, he would give the family of the little girl some foodstuffs to avert starvation. Since the foodstuffs would not be adequate, the man would pay a discounted bridewealth in addition to the foods. In most cases, the girl would be too young to marry at this point, so, she would continue to live with her parents until the onset of puberty. At puberty, she would then be escorted to her elderly husband. There were cases where the future husband would opt to take care of his would-be wife rather than permitting his in-laws to do that on his behalf. In such cases, the man was expected to abstain from having premature sexual relations with the little girl until the onset of puberty. Teenage girls could also be given away in marriage through *kuzvarira*, but, it was easier to arrange such a marriage for small girls because older girls would refuse to marry older men.

One of the advantages of *kuzvarira* was that no family that had a girl child would die of starvation because there was always a wealthy man who wanted an extra wife. But, there were challenges too. First, the girl would not give consent to such a marriage since she would be too young to understand what would be happening.

Second, Tabona Shoko notes that such marriage arrangements have back-fired because some girls refuse to marry older men in the modern Shona society.[8] Many times, such girls would run away from their families just before they are escorted to their elderly husbands. Sometimes they get impregnated by young men of their ages, and their families have to pay back what they would have received from the intended husband. Third, the system deprived innocent little girls of childhood playing and games. They were expected to quickly mature so that they could fulfill their marital obligations. Fourth, the age difference between the girl and the man was another setback. The old husband could easily order the underage wife around. Finally, some older men failed to satisfy their young women, sexually, and some of the wives ended up having extra-marital affairs.

Although the occurrence of *kuzvarira* marriages has been reported in modern times, they have become rare because of the condemnation that they have received from the government and other non-governmental pressure groups. In fact, The Native Marriages Ordinance of 1901 outlawed forced marriages although the practice of *kuzvarira* and other forced marriages continued for a long time, covertly.[9] In the modern Zimbabwe, marrying underage women is a criminal offense but instances of their occurrences have been reported.

## Kugara nhaka (Levirate and Sorority Marriages)

### *Levirate Marriage*

There are two forms of *kugara nhaka* marriages, namely, levirate and sororate. A levirate marriage takes place when a man dies leaving a sexually active woman and no adequate number of children. If that widow wants

8. Ibid., 26.

9. Schmidt, *Peasants, Traders, and Wives*, 111–12.

to remarry and remain in the family of her late husband she may opt for a brother, cousin or nephew of the dead husband. Some widows can choose not to remarry but to remain in their deceased husbands' homes by appointing one of their sons as their legal guardians.

The levirate marriage is supposed to take place on the day after the *Kurova Guva* ceremony that is usually performed at least six months after someone dies. This ceremony cleanses the spirit of the deceased and brings him back into the family as an ancestor. The widow is expected to remain chaste from the time of the death of her husband up to the *Kurova Guva* ceremony during which she is supposed to prove her faithfulness to the late husband by crossing one of his weapons. The weapon can be an ax, bow, and arrow, gun or a knobkerrie. That ceremony is known among the Shona as the *kudarika vuta* ceremony. *Kudarika vuta* means jumping over the weapon. It is believed that if the widow had been involved in some illicit sexual encounters during the period between the death of her husband and this ceremony, she would fall over the weapon, and that would be used as evidence that she had been unfaithful. It should be noted that nowadays, some widows refuse to perform the *kudarika vuta* ritual, not necessarily because they would have been unfaithful to their dead husbands, but just to show the community that the ritual is biased against women and violates their right to freedom.

After the *kudarika vuta* ceremony, the widow is required to choose a husband from the brothers and other qualified relatives of her late husband who would be sitting in a circle with the widow kneeling inside the circle and holding a bowl of water. Whoever the widow chooses, she washes his hands with the water from the bowl. Those contenders who are not interested in the widow may refuse to have their hands washed. If the widow has a son she may choose him, and by so doing, she is declaring that she is no longer interested in a sexual relationship but continuing to live in her late husband's home. If she chooses her elder son to be her guardian the widow is expected to remain chaste and celibate as long as she remains in the home of the deceased husband. Some elders argue that the widow's choice is not a surprise to the chosen man because the two would have agreed with each other in the period between the death of the husband and the *Kurova Guva* ceremony. Sometimes, other contenders participate in the ritual with the pre-knowledge of the widow's choice. A widow who just takes her choice by surprise may risk the man's rejection although that is not expected.

If the widow chooses to be inherited by one of the brothers or eligible relatives of her deceased husband, children that are born out of that wedlock belong to the dead brother. The new husband may marry another wife if he is not married at the time of the ritual, or may decide to stick to the widow of his brother. Levirate marriages serve some purposes. The widow and her children automatically find a protector and provider because the majority of Shona women were not gainfully employed, and the death of the breadwinner would robe the widow and her children of a decent livelihood. Second, if the widow and her late husband had not begotten an adequate number of children, then, the levirate marriage provided more children. Third, levirate marriages ensured that the wife kept her part of the marital obligation of begetting children since bridewealth would have been paid. If part of the bridewealth is still outstanding at the time of the death of the original husband, the new husband has to pay the arrears.

Fourth, the children that were begotten before the death of the first husband would have the same totem and *blood* with the children born out of the levirate marriage.[10] Furthermore, Aylward Shorter contents that levirate marriages cater for the surplus women in the community because of the high mortality rate of men.[11] The substantial death rate of men in Africa could have been caused by tribal wars and attacks by wild animals during hunting. Sixth, this arrangement makes it easier for the widow to satisfy her sexual needs because, in some cases, it is hard for widows and single mothers to find a husband. Finally, the new husband does not need to pay another bridewealth, but will be required to pay the arrears that existed at the time of the death of the formal husband.

There are challenges to both men and women who are involved in this marital arrangement. First, the new husband might contract the same disease that would have killed his brother, if it were a sexually transmitted disease. Second, sometimes the brothers, cousins, and nephews who may contend for the widow might be limited, so, the widow may end up making a choice out of desperation. Third, where prior arrangements are not made by the widow with one of the contenders, the ritual forces the two into a marriage first, then, love is supposed to follow, which might not happen at all. Fourth, the levirate marriage increases the responsibilities of the new husband if he has a family of his own at the time of the ritual.

## Sororate Marriage

Among the Shona, sororate marriages can be divided into two categories, namely, *chimutsamapfihwa* and *chigadzamapfiwa*.

---

10. The traditional Shona believed that children of the same parents had the same type of blood. They did not worry about blood groups and DNA.

11. Shorter, *African Culture and the Christian Church*, 173,

## Chimutsamapfihwa[12]

If a married woman dies prematurely, after her husband has paid most of the bridewealth or if she leaves behind young children, it is the responsibility of her family of origin to offer her young sister or her brother's daughter to the widower as a wife. This arrangement is done for three significant reasons. First, if the deceased wife had not satisfactorily fulfilled her responsibility of bearing an adequate number of children, this arrangement ensured the birth of more children on behalf of the deceased sister or aunt. Consequently, the father of the deceased wife would not be asked to return some of the bridewealth to enable the widower to get another wife. Second, if the dead wife has left young children, her sister would be the best person to take care of them, rather than an entirely strange woman that the man might end up marrying. Third, the *chimutsamapfiwa* marriage makes it easier for the widower to find another wife, usually a young one.

## Chigadzamapfihwa[13]

The bearing of children is a religious responsibility among the Shona. According to John S. Mbiti, in Africa, failure to beget children is a disgrace, and is worse than committing genocide.[14] No marriage could be said to be consummated until a sufficient number of children are born. Unfortunately, there is no stipulated number of children that can be said to be adequate. The adequacy of children depends on the husband and his extended family. Children are vital because they have the responsibility to take care of their elderly parents, and more importantly, to perform the *Kurova Guva* ceremony that transforms their deceased parents into ancestors. John S. Mbiti has put it succinctly as follows: "A person who, therefore, has no descen-

12. *Chimutsamapfihwa* is a Shona compound word that comes from *chimutsa*, meaning the one who revives, and *mapfihwa*, meaning the three stones that are used to balance the pot when cooking. So, the *chimutsamapfihwa* means the one who revives the cooking. In the Shona culture, cooking is the preserve of the wife. So, if the wife dies, it is assumed that there is no cooking taking place in that home. The cooking can also mean the sexual act that ceases to be performed as soon as the wife dies. Therefore, the new wife revives both the physical and the symbolic cooking.

13. *Chigadzamapfihwa* comes from two Shona words, *chigadza*, meaning the one who prepares or places the pot on the cooking stones, and *mapfihwa*, meaning the stones that balance the pot when cooking. So, *chigadzamapfihwa* refers to the one who comes to ensure the continual physical cooking and sexual intercourse by consummating the marriage through bearing children. A marriage in which there were no children was not expected to last.

14. Mbiti, *African Religions and Philosophy*, 107.

dants in effect quenches the fire of life, and becomes forever dead since his line of physical continuation is blocked if he does not get married and bear children."[15] However, there are times when married couples do not have any children because of one reason or another. If that happens, traditionally, the culprit would be the wife. Her parents are expected to offer the son-in-law another wife, ordinarily, her young sister, cousin or niece. This new wife would become the second wife of the same husband, and would bear children for her barren sister or aunt. But, if the sister or aunt would have left young children or no children at all, the new wife would be the sole wife of the widower.

If it were discovered that it was the husband who could not bear children, then his aunt, with the consent of family elders, would ask the young brother of the husband to have a clandestine sexual affair with his brother's wife to bear children for him. Although this was the male equivalent of the *chigadzamapfihwa*, the man was never referred to by that term because this arrangement was a family secret.

Sororate marriages benefited both the widower and the new wife. Usually, the arrangement gave families an opportunity to marry off their daughters who seem to have failed to get married as soon as they expected. There are cases where contenders have to struggle to win the widower's choice. If the son-in-law is wealthy, a sororate marriage enables the father-in-law to revive the marriage and relationship that could have ended with the death of their daughter.

Sororate marriages do have their challenges just like other types of marriage. First, although some prospective wives are pleased about the arrangements, there are times when very young girls, who are not old enough to give their consent are forced into sororate marriages. Second, the age difference between the new wife and the husband might act against the freedom of the new wife. Third, sometimes the father-in-law is tempted not to offer their best daughter to the son-in-law, so, he ends up getting a head-strong wife. Finally, the new wife could be affected by the same disease that would have killed her sister or aunt, if it was a sexually transmitted disease, such as HIV and AIDS.

In some cases, both levirate and sororate marriages in Africa lead to polygyny.[16] The institution of polygyny has been condemned by Westerners

15. Ibid., 130.

16. Polygyny is a compound word from two Greek words, *"poly"* meaning many, and *"gune,"* meaning woman. Therefore, the word polygyny means a marriage in which a man has more than one wife. A marriage in which a woman has more than one husband is known as polyandry, from the two Greek terms, *"poly,"* meaning many, and *"andros,"* meaning man. The word polygamy, meaning many marriages, can refer to

as an African institution that was built on lust and male selfishness. Aylward Shorter disagrees with the above perspective for the reason that African men had other avenues where they could satisfy their lusts, for example, adulterous unions and concubinage.[17] For him, there are many other legitimate reasons for polygyny which fall beyond the scope of this project.

One of the questions that the need for children in Shona marriages raise is that of child adoption. Why don't barren Shona couples adopt children? Child adoption is foreign to the Shona kinship system. The Shona believe that a child should have the same totem and blood with the father. That does not mean that the Shona do not take care of other people's children—they do. Children can grow up under other people's guardianship, but they can never be formally adopted as the guardian's children. In the past, most orphans would be cared for by either maternal or paternal relatives but, no one ever thought of formally adopting the children as his or her own. It was rare for a stranger to be the guardian of an orphaned kid because it was the responsibility of that kid's relatives to take care of him or her. Those orphans whose parents were not known or had no known relatives would be taken care of by orphanages, or even become street urchins. Most childless Shona couples would rather remain childless than formally adopting a child.

## Avenging Spirit (Ngozi) Marriage

For one to understand the avenging spirit marriages one has to understand the significance and pervasiveness of such spirits among the Shona. *Ngozi* is the most pervasive and horror-striking good spirit among the Shona. It refers to the spirit of a deceased person, who would have been treated badly in life or would have been murdered, which comes back to the perpetrator or the perpetrator's family, demanding justice and compensation for the wrong done and the loss suffered. Any murdered person, including those whose deaths were a result of an accident, deceased ill-treated mother, and an aborted child can come back to haunt the perpetrator's family as *ngozi*. There are several ways in which spirits of the dead become avenging spirits. Some spirits do that on their own accord without any promptings from their living relatives. Some spirits are invoked by their living relatives so that they come back to seek justice. The relatives do that by going to the grave of the deceased person and offer tobacco or libation to the spirit of the dead and then instruct it to go after the perpetrators of its death or injustice and seek justice. Some groups of Shona people immunize their children at birth so

---

either polygyny or polyandry.

17. Shorter, *African Culture and the Christian Church*, 173.

that their spirits can become *ngozi* if they are murdered or treated unjustly. Some living relatives may plant a tree at the grave of the deceased relative with the expectation that at a certain stage of the tree's growth, each leaf that falls off the tree, would cause sickness, bad luck or even death in the family of the wrong-doer. Some relatives visit a traditional medical practitioner to be assisted in invoking the spirit of the dead so that it would go to demand justice and compensation from the perpetrator or his/her family.

The symptoms of the attacks that are caused by avenging spirits include but are not limited to the following: recurring bad luck, failure to get a job, marriage partner, or offspring, being victimized by robbers, insatiable desire to cause harm to others, harming people intentionally or accidentally, several unexplainable deaths in the family, and sicknesses that cannot be explained medically. Sometimes, the undertakers may fail to fit the deceased person's body into the coffin, or they may fail to lift up the coffin. The perpetrator may see the ghost of the killed person or hear voices of the deceased asking why the perpetrator killed him or her. In some cases, someone in the wrong-doer's family may become possessed by the spirit of the killed person and demands compensation. The Shona fear the avenging spirit because of several reasons. First, it attacks family members of the perpetrator, indiscriminately, starting with those who have no awareness of what happened. So, no one is spared. Second, the avenging spirits unlike other spirits, cannot be exorcized. Third, the only solution is to appease the *ngozi* is by paying compensation to the family of the victim. Usually, there is no negotiation as to how much compensation is to be paid because what the avenging spirit wants is supposed to be paid. Last, when it comes to the payment of compensation to the family of the victim, all family members contribute because in most cases, the perpetrator cannot afford to pay it alone.

There are many types of avenging spirits that include the spirit of the offended mother, ill-treated vagabond, murdered person, the spirit of an improperly buried wife, particularly one whose burial is not authorized by her family of origin because bridewealth has not been paid in full, and others. The avenging spirit of an ill-treated or murdered vagabond or alien is the most devastating. A vagabond is usually a homeless person who has refused to take personal responsibility for himself and his family. Most of them are not married though far past the marrying stage. Most vagabonds are very poor and dirty because of self-neglect. Sometimes even young people can become vagabonds. If such a person is ill-treated, then his spirit would come back to seek justice. Connected to the vagabond, is the spirit of the unjustly treated alien. Most of these were mostly people coming from Malawi, Zambia, and Mozambique in search of work on the mines, commercial farms, or in the rural areas of Zimbabwe. Some people would employ them to do menial work at their homes or their farms. Mostly, these would be young men. If these are not remunerated as per agreement and then the person dies, there would be a serious *ngozi* seeking justice and compensation.

Among the Shona, life is sacred and it should never be taken away for any reason, even by an accident. If that happens, the spirit of the dead person would come back to demand justice and compensation. The compensation can be in the form of cows, money, and young girls. Young girls are demanded by the avenging spirits who would have been murdered before they were married. The young girl would become the wife of the avenging spirit. There were several ways in which the *ngozi* spirit would make use of such a wife. First, the spirit would allow one of its living brothers or nephews to inherit the wife and bear children for it. This was crucial because without children of its own the *ngozi* could not become an ancestor. So, the children born out of that wedlock belong to the dead person, which qualifies it to become an ancestor. Second, some avenging spirits would require the wife to remain in her parents' home but she would lead a celibate and chaste life. She would become the wife of the *ngozi,* which is believed to drive away would-be lovers of the woman. Some women would get possessed by the *ngozi* whenever another man tried to be intimate with them and she would severely beat them up. Some avenging spirits would allow their compensatory wives to get married to men that they loved but the bridewealth paid for them would be used by the *ngozi's* parents or relatives.

Whether the existence of the avenging spirit is a reality or a figment of the Shona's imagination, the majority of the Shona people are horrified by it. The majority of Shona people would try to pay compensation if they are told that their tribulations are a result of an avenging spirit. Even if the perpetrator is jailed for his actions, his family also compensates the family of the murdered person to appease the spirit of the deceased. The biggest challenge of *ngozi* marriage is that very young girls who cannot give their consents to such arrangements are sometimes forced into such marriages. Although the government of Zimbabwe has outlawed child marriages, some people are still tempted to do it because of the fear of avenging spirits. Even in cases where girls gave their consent to becoming the *ngozi's* wives, it is just weird to be the wife of a spirit. The spirit may deprive the young woman of ever engaging with males intimately throughout her life, which is a violation of her right to free association.

## Mapoto (Co-habitation)

*Mapoto* is an illicit and temporary marriage between two consenting adults for the sake of satisfying their immediate sexual and economic needs.[18] *Mapoto* marriages were rampant in mining, farming, and town compounds where married men lived alone while working there. According to Alois S. Mlambo, the arrival of the British and the subsequent establishment of their rule and capitalist labor markets enticed young males to the urban areas in search of gainful employment. That impacted adversely on the women who were left alone in the rural areas where they became responsible for the duties that previously belonged to men such as herding cattle, building houses, and so on. When some of the women could not produce as much as they would have done together with the assistance of their husbands, they too left the countryside to join the capitalist labor market.[19] Since the wages were not adequate some of those women ventured into prostitution and *mapoto* arrangements if they were not married.[20]

Mapoto became a lucrative marriage venture by some unmarried Shona women because most Shona workers' families lived in the rural homes to which the workmen would occasionally visit, usually, once per month. Of course, *mapoto* marriages were not a monopoly of married men because some single men also practiced them. Normally, most women who practiced *mapoto* were single or single mothers. This co-habitation is still being practiced by some Shona men and women. Both the man and the woman who are involved in such a union know very well that it is temporary and illegitimate because no bridewealth has been paid or is intended to be paid for the woman. The importance and significance of bridewealth will be discussed in chapter 3. At times, children are born out of such a union, and some *mapoto* marriages become legitimate as soon as bridewealth is paid.

One of the advantages of such a marriage is that the couple can quench their sexual desires without being committed to a long term union. Second, both parties get some benefits out of the illicit union: the man gets unlimited sexual favors, and someone to do his household chores for free, and the woman gets sexual satisfaction and financial support. Third, there are times when such unions develop into official marriages, and that is good for both partners. The disadvantages are many. First, the union is illegitimate and not recognized by the families of both the man and the woman. Second, some

18. *Mapoto* is a Shona word that comes from the singular word *poto*. Shona elders do not quite know the origin of the phrase *"kuchaya Mapoto,"* meaning to beat the pots. Symbolically, pots can refer to the sexual activity that the couple would be involved in.

19. Mlambo, *A History of Zimbabwe*, 114.

20. Ibid.

women who are involved in such unions are abused by their husbands or partners because their families are not concerned about whatever happens to them. Third, if *mapoto* is being practiced by a married man, it can destroy that man's family. Fourth, it dehumanizes the people who are involved in it since the Shona society demeans such people. Fifth, it degrades the integrity of the legitimate marriages. Finally, it may spread sexually transmitted diseases.

## Small Housing

Small housing is a recent form of marriage that has become almost the norm for some wealthy men in Zimbabwe. A small house is a woman who is involved sexually, on a more or less permanent basis, with a married man, clandestinely. Small houses live alone with their children if they do have any, in houses or apartments being rented out for them by their illicit partners. Small housing is different from both *mapoto* and polygyny because the small house lives by herself but is occasionally visited by the man, and no bridewealth is expected to be paid. The man takes care of the woman and her children's needs if she has any. Children can be born out of that union, and their existence is kept a secret from the man's formal wife, relatives, and official children.

Some small housing unions may eventually become official marriages if bridewealth is paid. One of its advantages is that it enables married men who cannot be involved in polygyny, to be involved in some form of polygamous union. Some small houses get money to send their children to colleges from their partners. Since it is hard for single mothers to get married in Zimbabwe, the small housing institution helps women to quench their sexual desires without becoming whores or prostitutes. Furthermore, married men whose official wives are barren can have children born to them by their small houses. Those who need male children and cannot get them from their legitimate wives can try their luck with small houses. Some men whose legal wives deny them conjugal rights can satisfy their sexual needs with the small houses. Since sex is discouraged when the woman is in menstrual periods, when advanced in pregnancy, and a couple of weeks after childbirth, small houses help men who cannot stay away from sex during those periods. One other good thing is that small housing unions can develop into legitimate marriages as soon as bridewealth is paid.

Small housing has its own challenges. It is illegal and illegitimate. The small house can be sued for damages by the official wife. Children that are born out of wedlock are looked down on in the Shona society, and they do not enjoy the protection and love of their father since he comes to their mother's home, occasionally and cannot associate with them publicly. Besides, small house unions can lead to the spread of sexually transmitted disease since both the involved man and the woman are not legally bound to have one partner at a time. Furthermore, such unions destroy marriages and families if discovered by the official wife. Finally, small houses deprive their relatives of bridewealth because their partners are not recognized as legitimate husbands.

## Polygamy

Polygamy is one of the significant marriage institutions that deserve a brief exploration at this juncture. The debate about polygamy has to involve a clarification of the terms that are used in connection with it. The word polygamy comes from two Greek words, *polu,* meaning, many and *gamos,* meaning marriage. Hence, polygamy means *many marriages,* either by a man or woman. The term does not define the African phenomenon of polygamy, accurately. Technically, the marriage union in which one man has more than one wife is known as *polygyny,* a compound word from two Greek words, *polu,* meaning many, and *gune,* meaning woman. Another important word is *polyandry* that comes from the Greek words, *polu,* meaning many, and *andros,* meaning husband. Therefore, *polyandry* refers to a situation in which a woman marries multiple men at the same time, and is not normally practiced in Africa. So, what Africans practice is *polygyny* although the term *polygamy* will be used in this writing for practical reasons.

There are three types of marriages in Zimbabwe although only two are legally recognized. The legally unrecognized, most popular, and oldest is the *Unregistered Customary Union* that was in existence before the arrival of the British in 1890.[21] The payment of bridewealth validates and legalizes such unregistered unions. Men who are married by unregistered marriage unions can marry as many wives as they want if they can pay bridewealth for them. Moreover, the *Unregistered Customary Union* does not stipulate the minimum age of marital consent. The second type of marriage is the *Customary Marriages Act, Chapter 5:07.* This type of marriage is validated by the exchange of marriage vows by the couple before the district marriage officer, the woman's guardian or his representative, the chief or headman or village head of the guardian, or their representative. It should be noted that the woman's guardian may not give his consent unless a substantial

21. According to Felix Share, about 84 percent of Zimbabwe's customary marriages are unregistered ("84pc of Zim Marriages Unregistered," *Herald* [Harare], June 6, 2013).

amount of bridewealth has been paid. The minimum age of the woman who can legally contract this marriage is not clear. The man can marry as many wives as he wants or can afford. Sometimes he has to seek the permission of his first wife if he wants to take a second wife. However, if the first wife refuses to grant that permission, the husband can still go ahead and take another wife. The third type of marriage is called *The Marriage Act, Chapter 5:11*. This type requires one man and woman union as long as it stands. It is administered by magistrates, their officers, and other qualified people such as church ministers. Most Christian churches in Zimbabwe promote this type of marriage. The minimum age for the woman has just been raised from sixteen to eighteen, and that of the man remains at eighteen. So, Zimbabweans can choose the kind of marriage they would want to use from the those above. Although more couples are now choosing the *Marriage Act, Chapter 5:11*, there are some who go for the other two.

Traditionally, the Shona society permitted polygamy, and it continues to do so up to now. To an outsider, the most common but shameful reason for polygamy is the African men's insatiable lust. Although lust could be one of the causes, it is erroneous to think that it was the only and most significant reason. Polygamy served economic, religious, social, and other purposes in the traditional Shona society. Traditionally, the Shona relied on farming, hunting, trade, and bridewealth for their economic well-being. Since they did not have modern farming or mining technology, they depended on the labor that their wives and children provided. More work was needed for gold panning too. The more wives and children a man had the greater the food and gold output. The fact that there were higher infant and maternal mortality rates did not help the situation. Couples had to replace the so many children who died in infancy and women who died in labor.

Connected to the above point was the issue of bridewealth. If a man had more wives, he would perhaps have more daughters, and he was likely to acquire more bridewealth when they married. The reception of more bridewealth increased the family wealth, particularly, the cattle. More cattle would provide more milk, meat, and hides for the family. Consequently, there was a need to have more wives so that they could bear more children.

Among the Shona, marriage is a religious obligation that all able-bodied people should uphold. It is through marriage that a man's name is perpetuated, and his spirit achieves immortality as an ancestor. One of the qualifications to become an ancestor is for a man to have children that include at least one son. Boys are responsible for performing the cleansing ritual that enables a person's spirit to become an ancestor. In the past, if a couple failed to get a son, the simplest solution was for the man to get another wife. More sons had to be born because some of them died during hunting and fighting.

Some other religious issues influenced Shona men to marry more than one wife. Sexual activities were tabooed during a woman's menstrual periods, and when she was advanced in pregnancy, and a few weeks after the birth of a child. During those times, the man could satisfy his sexual desire by using the services of other wives. Levirate and sororate marriages also forced men to have more than one wife. In most cases, polygamy was a societal responsibility that was designed to cushion widows and their children from the challenges of life without a breadwinner. Although some widows could marry again, for others, it was not easy to find another husband after the death of the first.

Polygamy discouraged divorce because a man could continue to live with his wives even if he had ceased to love them. The man would not compel any of his wives to have sex with him because there was almost always a woman who could provide that service willingly. Those women who for one reason or another ceased to have an interest in sex were not divorced or forced to have sex. The husband simply married other women who catered to him sexually while taking care of those women who were no longer sexually active.

Of course, there were challenges in polygamous unions, some of which are similar to those that are found in monogamous marriages. There were quarrels, fighting, jealousy, favoritism, and hatred. Sometimes the man could not satisfy all his wives sexually, and that could force some of the women to find illicit lovers. The age difference between the man and some of his wives would be too significant to the extent that some of his wives appeared as if they were his children. Also, it has been argued that polygamy encouraged some men to become lazy since women and children would do most of the work in the fields. Moreover, mostly wealthy men could afford to pay bridewealth for more than one wife. So, there were men who were deprived of marrying more wives because of their economic challenges, and some of them could have envied those men who could afford.

Polygamy has been demonized by both the Christian missionaries and the British settlers as uncivilized, inconsistent with God's command, and the oppression of women. As a result of that condemnation, the majority of Shona men have abandoned it. But, that is not the end of the story because some of them have replaced it by the small housing practice. One of the significant advantages of having a small house rather than taking a second wife is that the man appears civilized and continues to be in communion with his church.

Polygamy is one of the marriage institutions that need revisiting by African scholars, theologians, churches, pastors, and governments. The timing is right because Westerners are battling with marital issues that they used to condemn in the past, such as homosexuality. If the West is contemplating the legalization of gay marriages after centuries of demonizing them, then Africans must also think of revisiting the issue of polygamy. This suggestion does not imply that the two phenomena are the same and therefore, comparable, but that cultures are dynamic and diverse and because of that no one has the authority to dictate what other people should accept as cultural normativity.

## Comments

The fact that marriage is crucial in any human society that tries to evade extinction cannot be over-stated. The Shona people had a variety of marriages that were put in place to enable everyone who wished to get married find a spouse. No free Shona person is deprived of the right to marry. Be that as it may, it should be noted that the payment of bridewealth plays a significant role in all Shona marriages. In fact, bridewealth is a common phenomenon in Africa and "is a typical feature of the African marriage."[22] It legitimates both the marriage and the children born of that marriage.

Of all the forms of marriage among the Shona people, *kukumbira* is upheld as the noblest, most legitimate, and most desired. *Kukumbira* is the form of marriage that is highly considered even by other religious traditions such as Christianity. Although there are many reasons that compel the Shona people to regard *kukumbira* marriage with high esteem, the bridewealth factor plays a critical role in that. *Kukumbira* ensures that no woman is snatched away from her family home for the purpose of marriage unless the man pays a substantial amount of bridewealth first. The family head of the woman has more bargaining powers if the woman is not yet pregnant and is living with them at the time of bridewealth negotiations. So, *kukumbira* allows the family head to hold on to the woman until the would-be son-in-law pays his due. In their refusal to release their daughters before the son-in-law pays bridewealth, some family heads are not interested in the welfare of the girls, but in receiving bridewealth first. However, like any other significant institutions, bridewealth is open to abuse. Chapter 3 will deal with some of the ways in which bridewealth has been abused, and how it has become an impediment to the total emancipation of Shona women.

22. Shorter, *African Culture and the Christian Church*, 167.

# Chapter 3

## Bridewealth and Domestic Violence
among the Shona

### Introduction

AT THIS JUNCTURE, a recap of what has been covered so far is warrant-
ed. Chapter 1 dealt with domestic violence among the Shona people of
Zimbabwe by exploring the experiences, statistics, causes, and types of domestic violence that happen within the marriage setup. Although both men
and women can be victims or perpetrators of domestic violence, chapter
1 was fundamentally concerned with the violence that is perpetrated by
husbands against wives. The same chapter also briefly stated that one of the
leading causes of domestic violence in Zimbabwe is the cultural practice of
bridewealth.

Chapter 2 explored the various types of marriage among the Shona
of Zimbabwe and also mentioned, on several occasions, the centrality and
significance of bridewealth among the Shona. The same chapter alluded to
the fact that some types of marriages such as *kukumbira* are more respected
than others by the Shona people because they give leverage to the parents
or relatives of the bride during the bridewealth negotiations. *Kukumbira* is
the most highly regarded form of marriage because the Shona believe that
it gives evidence to the high moral standards of both the woman concerned
and her family.

Chapter 3 starts by exploring the Shona kinship system that gave
rise to the practice of bridewealth and assesses the marriage institution in

which bridewealth plays a central role. It then discusses the rights that a husband acquires after paying bridewealth and evaluates the contribution of bridewealth in the intensification, escalation, and perpetuation of domestic violence against Shona women by their husbands. As shall be observed later, in the past, bridewealth had mechanisms that were intended to prevent the wanton abuse of wives by their husbands, which are no longer available now. Be that as it may, the practice was never designed to place women on par with men, and it made Shona women vulnerable to domestic violence. Although I am aware of the fact that there are many other cultural practices that promote the subordination, exploitation, abuse, and subjugation of the Shona women in the marriage setup, the payment of exorbitant bridewealth tops the list. Other cultural practices that contribute to the abuse of women in a marriage structure include, but are not limited to the age difference between the wife and husband; the myth of the love potion; belief in witchcraft; the practice of polygyny; demand for woman virginity; child marriages; among others. However, this book only deals with bridewealth, which the Shona and Ndebele call *rovoro/pfuma* and *lobola*, respectively.[1]

## Shona Kinship Systems

To understand the origins and significance of bridewealth among the Shona people and how it causes the subjugation, oppression, abuse, and exploitation of women, one needs to understand the Shona kinship system that gave birth to bridewealth, and to appreciate the marriage institution in which bridewealth plays a critical role. Many researchers who tried to understand the practice of bridewealth among African people in isolation of the African kinship systems and marriage institutions ended up misrepresenting and misinterpreting what they observed and heard. Some of them ended up equating the payment of bridewealth to the purchase of a wife, an assumption that was not only erroneous but also bigoted.

According to A. R. Radcliffe-Brown, two people, are kin when one is descended from the other, or both are from a common forebear.[2] Marshall W. Murphree, who carried out research among the Shona people called the *Budjga* notes that "the *Budjga* are divided into exogamous patrilineal totemic clans, which are identified by the clan name and sub-clan name. The

1. *Rovoro* is the Shona word for bridewealth and the Ndebele equivalent is *lobola*, which has become more popular in Zimbabwe. The words *rovoro*, *lobola*, and bridewealth will be used interchangeably throughout this chapter. The Ndebele are the second largest tribe in Zimbabwe and they occupy the region known as Matabeleland with their capital Bulawayo, which happens to be Zimbabwe's second largest city.

2. Radcliffe-Brown, "Introduction," in *African Systems of Kinship and Marriage*, 3.

significance of the clan is two-fold: it regulates marriage and it provides the genealogical framework for the politically dominant lineages."[3] The same kinship structure can be said to be true of other Shona clans.

The Shona society contains an extensive web of relationships, and offspring is closely related to both the father and mother's lineages.[4] The biggest unit of inclusion is the clan that comprises of interrelated people who claim to have the same descent. A clan is followed by the sub-clan division that is made up of a more related group of people. The lineage and sub-lineage then follow under the clan and sub-clan. In the past, Shona people who belonged to the same clan were related through totem and lived in the same locality under their chief. Although the people who lived in the same clan were related in one way or the other, most clans also allowed strangers, who are known in Shona as *vatorwa*, to live among them. Some of the *vatorwa* were people who would have joined the clan as political refugees, and as sons-in-law although the latter migration was discouraged by the Shona people. There were also strangers who joined new clans in search of greener pastures. It should be noted that some aliens took up their hosts' totems so that they could be more accepted by their hosts. However, most strangers, if not all, retained their totems and because of that they could intermarry with the members of the host clan.

A totem is derived from an animal or other natural phenomena such as fire, water, animal leg, and others. Totems are sub-divided into sub-totems or *chidawo*. So, people who belong to the same totem are considered to be related, but they are deemed to be more closely-related if they have the same sub-totem. The totem can be the same, for instance, lion, but there are several lion sub-totems such as Murambwi, Sigauke, Charumbira, and Mhazi. The relationship becomes closer if the people involved belong to the same extended family. The nucleus family is the smallest entity as far as kinship is concerned. Marriage between persons of the same totem or sub-totem is considered incest among the Shona. A man or woman is obliged to marry someone from a different totem or sub-totem although there were rare instances when close relatives were allowed to get married. In such particular circumstances a ritual known as *kuchekana ukama* (cutting off relationship) in which a white cow was sacrificed to the ancestors of the families concerned and the clan was performed.[5] I think that the choice of the color of the cow was deliberately intended to discourage people from marrying relatives because white cows were rare. However, some people now ignore the

---

3. Murphree, *Christianity and the Shona*, 27.

4. Holleman, *The Pattern of Hera Kinship*, 16.

5. Daneel, *Old and New in Southern Shona Independent Churches*, 49.

totemic taboos and marry spouses with the same totems as theirs although it is never encouraged.

## The Shona Marriage Contract

Although the Shona marriage types have been dealt with in Chapter 2, a brief summary of the meaning, significance, and process of the Shona marriage contract suffices here. Marriage is a crucial institution among the Shona. Johan Fredrik Holleman who studied and lived among the Hera Shona of the then Charter District, now Chikomba, from 1945 to 1948 describes the Shona marriage contract as "essentially an agreement between two families in which the individual interest of the groom and bride, though implicitly or formally recognized, are but a subordinate element of the wider dominating interests of their families."[6] In concurrence with that A. R. Radcliffe-Brown has defined the same phenomenon as "an alliance between the two bodies of kin based on their common interest in the marriage itself and its continuance, and in the offspring of the union, who will be, of course, kin of both the two kin groups."[7]

Both definitions capture the heart of the Shona marriage contract, procedure, and significance. It is true that marriage among the Shona is a clan, lineage, extended family, and nuclear-family affair. Although the individuals who are directly involved as husband and wife have their rights and expectations when entering their marriage, they know quite well that they are also an embodiment of the whole clan's or lineage's interests. The fruits of their marriage, particularly the children, benefit their clans and families in much the same way that they benefit the parents.

The purpose of marriage among the Shona is to create a new family unit by bearing children who automatically become members of the wider genealogical grouping.[8] It is imperative for each clan or lineage to bear children because that is the surest way to ensure its continuity. As has been said above, in the past, one of the critical marriage restrictions was the forbiddance of marriage between men and women who were related by totem, sub-totem, blood, and marital relationships. Any violation of that was considered incest. So, each kinship group had to get wives or husbands for its marriageable children from another kinship group. The biggest challenge was that each time a girl was married; her clan lost a daughter in her because she had to move from her original home and join her husband's

---

6. Holleman, *Shona Customary Law,* 73.

7. Radcliffe-Brown, "Introduction," 46.

8. Holleman, *Shona Customary Law,* 153.

clan. Such losses could have been abated if the direct exchange of women for marriage purposes were allowed. Unfortunately, the direct exchange of women for the wedding purposes was not encouraged among the Shona because of several reasons.

First, the direct exchange of women for marriage purposes demanded a double coincidence of wants. There was to be a constant supply of men and women of marriageable ages in the interested clans or kinship groups, and that was not always the case. Second, the direct exchange of women would have undermined the interests and rights of the men and women involved in such marriages because their choices of marriage partners would be limited. Although both the boy and the girl were supposed to be subordinate to the rights and interests of the clan and extended family, the Shona society had great respect for their children's free choices of marriage partners. Third, the Shona knew that love was one of the fundamental ingredients of a successful marriage, and the direct exchange of women would not promote the free expression of one's love. It would be like, "if you marry my sister, I will marry yours." Fourth, exchange marriages would complicate the Shona kinship system. It would make son-in-laws and father-in-laws on both sides.

Of course, there were rare and exceptional cases when the direct exchange of women for marriage purposes was allowed, but it was never the norm. The Shona derogatorily referred to that type of marriage as *matengana gudo* (baboon trade). Such a marriage would be allowed at the insistence of the man and woman who were involved, but in some cases, it would not be in the best interest of their families. So, if the direct exchange of women was not encouraged, there had to be a flexible way to compensate the families that lost their daughters to marriage. That compensation would then allow the receiving families to look for wives for their sons from other clans. That was the beginning of bridewealth.

## Bridewealth, Then and Now

Marthinus L. Daneel identifies bridewealth as, "the most tenacious" of all Shona customs that was established because of the marriage taboos that were found within the kinship system.[9] Some pioneer Christian missionaries who did not understand its origins, meaning and significance savagely condemned bridewealth. According to Ngwabi Bhebe, Fr. Prestage S.J, who arrived in Zimbabwe before 1890 is believed to have denounced bridewealth as a practice that was indistinguishable, "from the purchase of a wife by a man for the purpose of begetting children, among whom the girls, when

---

9. Daneel, *Old and New in Southern Shona Independent Churches*, 248.

marriageable are disposed to obtain *lobola* which is used again to purchase other wives, the final object being to acquire position and substance through the possession of women and children."[10] Fr. Prestage missed the point when he referred to the practice as the purchase of a woman, which it was not and was never intended to be. Aeneas S. Chigwedere vehemently disagrees with that notion. He writes: ". . . African men do not buy their wives. They buy the services of their wives. If you hire me to build you a house, you have not bought me, but have bought my services."[11] Fr. Prestage was also off the target when he brought in the acquisition of position and substance through the possession of women and children as one of the chief goals of the Shona bridewealth and marriage. It is quite evident that Fr. Prestage had not given enough time to the study of the Shona kinship and marriage systems.

So, it is imperative at this juncture to explore the practice of bridewealth that Robin Fox has defined as "the payment of goods to the lineage of the bride" that are intended to give the man rights over the woman.[12] These rights will be discussed later in this chapter. The *Encyclopedia of Social and Cultural Anthropology* defines bridewealth as, "a marriage payment from the groom or his kin to the kin of the bride, usually to legitimate children of the marriage as members of the groom's lineage."[13] Of course, there is more to it than legitimatizing the children as shall be seen later.

Radcliffe-Brown defines bridewealth as "an indemnity or compensation given by the bridegroom to the bride's kin for the loss of their daughter."[14] These definitions complement each other. It is true that when a daughter is married her clan or family loses a woman it can never replace unless it is directly given another woman in exchange for its own or compensated for its loss so that the compensation can allow the losing lineage to acquire another woman from another clan. Since the direct exchange of women for marriage purposes was discouraged by the Shona, bridewealth acted as compensation or indemnity for the married woman. A married woman is considered lost because her reproductive and productive capacities now belong to her husband, his family, and clan.

According to Johan F. Holleman, the primary purpose of this transaction is the reproduction of a lineage through the bearing of male children who will give the lineage more numbers and female children who will be

10. Bhebe, *Christianity and Traditional Religion in Western Zimbabwe*, 112.

11. Chigwedere, *Lobola*, 13.

12. Fox, *Kinship and Marriage*, 119.

13. Bernard and Spencer, eds., *Encyclopedia of Social and Cultural Anthropology*, 597.

14. Radcliffe-Brown, "Introduction," 50.

exchanged for compensation that will be used to acquire women from other clans. Male children were needed to assure the family of more descent and to carry out the ancestral rituals that were necessary for the family's well-being and perpetuity. As hunters, men provided food for their families. Besides that, men were fighters, and it was their responsibility to protect the clan from enemies and wild animals. Of course, the importance of sons does not take anything away from daughters; they were paramount in their right as well. Female children were vital because the bridewealth that would be paid for them would make it possible for their brothers to marry thereby perpetuating the name of the family and clan. Holleman puts it as follows: "Thus a lineage, upon surrendering one of its marriageable females receives in exchange the means—typically a certain number of cattle—with which it can obtain a wife for its own reproductive purposes from another lineage."[15]

Bridewealth served many other purposes. According to William Rayner, it made the marriage contract solemn; it acted as an assurance of satisfactory treatment of the wife by her husband and bound the contracting families in mutual obligations. It was also believed to have given the institution of marriage dignity and stability, and dissuaded men from bullying or brutalizing their wives.[16] Bridewealth was not intended for the individual and personal use by the bride's father, but for the use of the family men who would use it to acquire women for the continual existence of the clan, and also increase the family's wealth. The beast of motherhood, the only cow that was given to the mother of the bride, would produce milk and offspring for the continual nourishment of the family.

Among the Shona, a son and daughter could be linked for bridewealth purposes. In the event of the daughter being married, the bridewealth paid for her would be used by the linked brother to pay bridewealth for his wife.[17] The Shona called both the sister and this system, *chipanda,* meaning bridewealth-linked sister. The sister who would have provided bridewealth for her brother commanded a lot of respect from the brother and his wife, and automatically became an arbitrator in domestic squabbles between her brother and his wife.[18] So, the wife was valued not only by her husband but by all the stakeholders and since bridewealth was scarce most men would not risk losing their wives.[19] According to Adam Kuper, among other Bantu-speaking people in Southern Africa the *chipanda* would be compensated

---

15. Holleman, *Shona Customary Law,* 148.
16. Rayner, *Tribe and Its Successors,* 56–58.
17. Holleman, *Shona Customary Law,* 44.
18. Ibid.
19. Gelfand, *The Genuine Shona,* 173.

by her brother through the provision of one of his daughters as a co-wife or daughter-in-law of the *chipanda* so that she would be subordinate to her, assist her in household chores, and bear children for her or her son.[20] Although among the Shona the *chipanda* was not compensated in such a manner, she too acquired some privileges from her brother and his wife and children. Of course, in the event of the *chipanda* failing to fulfill some of her marital obligations, she may ask for her brother's daughter to become a co-wife to her husband. However, the responsibility to provide a co-wife belonged to all the wife's brothers, not only the one who would have used his sister's bridewealth.

According to Holleman, there is evidence that originally, bridewealth among the Shona comprised between fifteen and twenty hoes, and about three goats. Before 1912, the standard rate was four head of cattle. Of the 600 marriages recorded at Range Office in Chikomba District, Chivhu, between 1907 and 1909, in 587 marriages the *rovoro* (bridewealth) was four head of cattle. By 1916 and 1924 the rate had gone up to eight and ten head of cattle respectively.[21] This increment is believed to have been caused by the increase in the number of cattle that the people had because of the end of the tribal wars in which many Shona clans lost cattle to raiders, particularly the Ndebele and other Shona people. The increase can also be attributed to the monetization of the economy by the British that made it easier for young men to find gainful employment, and would then pay their own bridewealth. Although this new situation was a welcome development, particularly to poor families, it eventually led to the privatization and commercialization of bridewealth.

Michael Bourdillon affirms the perspectives of both Holleman and Radcliffe-Brown concerning bridewealth. He observes that the traditional marriage among the Shona was primarily between families and fostered a relationship between wife-providers and wife- receivers.[22] It was an alliance between groups rather than between individuals. The bridewealth was negotiated by the heads of the two families or their representatives in the presence of a messenger. The bridewealth money or cattle were not intended for the individual benefit of the father of the bride. In many cases, sons had to be assisted by their father or paternal uncles to pay the bridewealth, or they would use the bridewealth from their sisters, to pay their own bridewealth.[23] That is why divorce was not easy among the Shona because all the

---

20. Kuper, *Wives for Cattles*, 34.
21. Holleman, *Shona Customary Law*, 161–63.
22. Bourdillon, *The Shona Peoples*, 37.
23. Ibid., 37–41.

stakeholders were to be involved since it would indirectly affect them too. Whenever there was a misunderstanding between the husband and wife, the first and obvious advice or preference of the relatives was for reconciliation, regardless of the reasons being cited for divorce.

Bridewealth was not a one-day payment, and it has remained the same up to today. As soon as the amount was agreed upon, and some of it paid, the woman had to consummate the union by getting pregnant and delivering children that were and are still an integral part of the Shona marriage. Childlessness and barrenness were seen as a curse. E. E. Evans-Pritchard described it very accurately when he wrote that "no woman is willingly childless—indeed to be childless is the worst misfortune that can befall her—and the vast majority of wives bear several children, though many die in infancy."[24]

## Bridewealth Rights and Shona Women Emancipation

Right from its inception bridewealth tended to benefit men more than it helped women. Although by its very nature, bridewealth had checks and balances, that to some extent, safeguarded the welfare of married women, it gave more rights to men than to women. It is a fact that some of these rights were not expressly communicated to the husband and the wife during the bridewealth negotiations, but both the man and the woman knew what their respective marital responsibilities and rights would be. To a larger extent, some Shona men use the acquired rights and privileges to subjugate, exploit, oppress, and abuse their wives. However, it should be noted that not all Shona men abuse their wives. It is also true that not all Shona men pay bridewealth, but most have been socialized to behave as if they have paid bridewealth even if they have not. Those who have not paid bridewealth claim to have almost the same rights over their wives just as those who would have paid bridewealth, either partly or entirely. This behavior could be the result of the Shona man's awareness that if the wife dies before he pays or finishes paying his bridewealth, it has to be paid before the family of the deceased woman can authorize the burial of their daughter. In Shona culture, the burial rituals of a deceased married woman should be presided over by members of her family of origin. If the burial rituals are not followed meticulously, the spirit of the dead woman would become an avenging spirit and would torment the family of the husband. So, sooner or later, the husband or his family will be compelled to pay bridewealth.

---

24. Evans-Pritchard, *The Position of Women in Primitive Societies*, 46.

## *Rights before Marriage*

The public announcement by a man of his intention to marry some woman and the beginning of bridewealth talks give the man some rights over the woman. Radcliffe-Brown calls the first set of rights that a man who proposes to marry a particular woman acquires, rights in *rem*, and these rights symbolize that the woman is now an intended spouse of a particular man. Rights in *rem* imply that the man could sue for damages inflicted upon his intended wife in certain circumstances.[25] Among the Shona, it is understood and assumed that as soon as the marriage negotiations start, the whole process will come to its logical conclusion with the successful wedding between the man and woman who are involved. It is also understood that the man will become the head of the family, and the woman will take her place in that family as the wife, mother, and food provider. Once the bridewealth negotiations start, divorce before the wedding is rare but possible. Such a divorce should be a result of a grievous issue such as infidelity, more on the side of the woman than of the man. Although, at this stage, the woman and the man are not husband and wife technically, they are given the respect that is reserved for married couples. Both should treat their in-laws with the utmost respect. They also should stop seeing other lovers if either of them had more than one.

The process of the payment of bridewealth is deliberately prolonged to allow the relatives of both the woman and man to assess the relationship. For that reason, no man is authorized to pay all the bridewealth on the same day or within a short period, even if he or his family is capable of doing so. There has to be a time for testing and assessing the durability and fruitfulness of the union. If the man proves to be abusive during this early stage the parents of the woman can challenge him and if he does not change his attitude they still have the option of returning his bridewealth and denying him the hand of their daughter. In like manner, if the woman proves to be socially undesirable, the man is free to ask for a refund of the bridewealth that he has paid for her or send her back to her paternal aunt for further instruction. Rights in *rem* represent one aspect of the total rights the man gains over the woman when she is finally delivered to him as his wife.

Although rights in *rem* do not give the future husband full-fledged rights over the would-be wife, such rights are biased against the woman. Even if apprehended, the man can get away with seeing other women at this stage, but the woman cannot. The woman's movements are monitored, but the man's are not. Although most men would hide their actual characters

25. Radcliffe-Brown, "Introduction," 12, 50.

to the would-be wives, some men may even harass their intended wives at this point.

## Miscellaneous Rights

Before the proper bridewealth negotiations start, there are many other small rights that the future husband has to pay for and then acquire. These are called *zvibinge* in Shona. He should pay for the permission to enter his father-in-law's home, and this is known as *kupinda mumusha*. Once that is done, he pays for the right to greet and then negotiate with his in-laws. The father-in-law must also be compensated for the instances that his daughter, as a child, played with his beard and that is known as *matekenya ndebvu*. The mother-in-law is not outdone at this stage because she too has to be given her *mapfukudza dumbu*. This compensation catered for two issues. First, it was for the discomfort the unborn baby might have caused her when she kicked about in her womb. Second, it also compensated the mother-in-law for the loss of girlish body shape as a result of the pregnancy and birth of her first child. Hence, in the past, *mapfukudza dumbu* was paid for first born daughters only. She is also compensated for the food that she cooks for the son-in-law's delegation. Usually, the son-in-law's delegation places the payment for the food in one of the empty plates after consuming the food. The amount placed in the plate might not be proportionate to the cost of the consumed food, but it is expected that the son-in-law's delegation offers a reasonable amount. In addition to that, she receives the balky of the groceries that the son-in-law's delegation brings. Usually, the son-in-law gets a list of all the required items a couple of weeks before the negotiations. The items may include: beer, cigarettes, cooking oil, meat, salt, sugar, flour, matches, and soft drinks, among others. The son-in-law should buy clothes known as *mabhachi* for the parents of his wife, usually suits, shoes, and a blanket.

Although the rights that the husband acquires at this stage do not directly affect the woman that he is in the process of marrying, they add to the total bridewealth bill, and might lead to resentment by the son-in-law and his delegation. Resentment by the husband might result in domestic violence. We have heard of married women that are constantly reminded that their bridewealth was so expensive and because of that they have to be loyal to the family of their husbands.

In addition to that, the fact that the woman is not expected to pay her husband's family in order to gain the same rights and privileges shows the extent that the wife and her family should feel indebted to the man. Furthermore, the money that the in-laws receive further compounds their reliance on and indebtedness to the son-in-law. It is weird that the wife's parents should seek compensation for having played with their daughter as a kid, or for the crimes that she committed as a fetus because that should fall under their responsibilities.

It should be noted that in the past, all those miscellaneous payments were not considered to be the bridewealth proper, and in the event of a divorce, the father-in-law was not required to refund those various fees. Although such payments are not refundable, they compound their obligation to the son-in-law. In the event of the abuse of their daughter by her husband, it is unlikely that they would challenge the son-in-law.

## Exclusive Sexual Rights

*Rugaba* or *rusambo* is paid for all services that the wife will provide except paternal rights. One of that entitlement the man gets is the exclusive sexual rights over the woman. Virgins fetch more *rugaba*. According to M. F. C. Bourdillon, only virgins had *rugaba* paid for them, in the past.[26] Among some Shona groups, the acquisition of these rights are explained to the son-in-law or his relatives by the aunt of the bride on the day on which the portion of the bridewealth that caters for that particular aspect is paid. Some Shona parents do not allow their daughter to join her husband's family on the day that *rugaba* is paid. She remains in her family's home for a couple of weeks after the payment, and she is then escorted to her husband's home by her aunt or young sisters. Some parents may demand that a church wedding be performed first before they allow their daughter to go and live with her husband and that demand may put a lot of pressure upon the son-in-law since he is expected to pay part of the *danga* (cattle) before the permission to have a church wedding can be granted.

However, at this stage, the husband, and his wife can start enjoying their conjugal rights. In the past, the first intimate encounter between the new husband and wife was expected to take place in the home of the bride so that her virginity could be confirmed. If the woman was found to be not a virgin, then, the *rugaba* payment had to be reduced to the shame and disgrace of the bride's family. Nowadays, the virginity of the bride does not need to be confirmed, although it is a question that is not left undecided. The lack of it will haunt the couple many years after the first night and might be used by abusive men to insult and subjugate their wives.

Once the husband has paid *rugaba*, he can sue for damages if his wife were to be involved in an illicit sexual affair with another man. In fact, in

26. Bourdillon, *The Shona Peoples*, 41.

the past, adultery was not a cause for divorce among most Shona groups because once the illegal lover had paid damages, the husband and wife were expected to remain together although it was not easy. Many couples survived such challenges. It is very interesting that if the man has paid part of the *rugaba*, the compensation for his wife's infidelity goes to him, not to her relatives. In such a case, the husband is the aggrieved party and should receive compensation because it is his exclusive sexual right to his wife that has been violated. Among the Shona, it seems that, before marriage, the reproductive capacity and system of the wife are jealously guarded and protected by her family, and after the payment of *rugaba* these are publicly and legally transferred to her husband.

The attainment of exclusive sexual rights is a significant step towards the consummation of the Shona marriage. The Shona, marriage is not consummated by the sexual act between the married couple, but with the birth of a sufficient number of children. It should be noted that in the past, the acquisition of exclusive sexual rights over one's wife did not grant the husband absolute paternal rights over the children born.[27] If the husband were to ill-treat his wife at this stage, her parents could reject the remaining bridewealth and would take back their daughter and then acquire her children. Likewise, if the woman failed to perform her expected duties such as cooking, washing, cleaning, farming or bearing children, the husband could as well send her back to her parents so that she would receive further instructions about her marital responsibilities.

If no portion of *danga* (cattle) has been paid at this point, the children born out of that union belong to the wife's relatives, particularly her father. However, to counteract a situation whereby a husband gains exclusive sexual rights over his wife but does not possess paternal rights, some men pay a small portion of *danga* on the day on which they pay their *rugaba* so that they also gain paternal rights simultaneously. Be that as it may, most Shona groups believe that once a man pays *rugaba*, there is a higher probability that he will eventually pay *danga* (cattle). So, that mere assumption gives the husband the desired paternal rights.

The payment of *rugaba* comes with a lot of challenges that may undermine the dignity and integrity of the woman. First, some men believe that the amount of *rugaba* is equivalent to the purchase of the wife's sexual organs and her reproductive capacity. Consequently, the woman is not expected to deny her husband his conjugal rights in any way, even though it may pose life-threatening dangers to her. Of course, there are men that are

---

27. Anthony Gittins, private lecture, Catholic Theological Union, Chicago, September 24, 2007.

denied conjugal rights by their wives, but they can beat them up or report them to their aunts, or even divorce them. To deny conjugal rights to one's husband without a believable impediment is tantamount to divorcing him. If that issue is reported to the relatives of the wife it causes so much embarrassment. In the end, some women end up engaging in sexual activities with their husbands against their will.

Second, *rugaba* trivializes the issue of marital rape. It is inconceivable for a Shona married woman, for whom *rugaba* was paid, to make allegations of a rape case against her husband. The report, if made, would scandalize not only the law enforcement agents, but also her parents who would have received *rugaba* from her husband. When a woman's parents accept *rugaba* from their son-in-law, the implicit contract is that their daughter will at all times make her body available to her husband alone (unless prevented by health issues) whenever he needs to be intimate with her. So, technically, a Shona man cannot rape his wife because he has paid for the right to have sex with her. By allowing her relatives to accept *rugaba* and spend it, a Shona woman is giving her unreserved consent to her husband's sexual advances whenever he deems it appropriate and reasonable. Of course, there are times when the wife is incapacitated to have sex with her husband in one way or the other, and any logical man is bound to respect that. But, any prolonged and unwarranted denial of conjugal rights to the husband may be dismissed by the man. If the wife insists on denying her husband his conjugal rights, the husband may beat her up so that she complies with his demands. In the past, such a wife would be sent back to her people, particularly her paternal aunt, for counseling. If she insisted, then divorce would be recommended, unless if the she allowed her husband to take a second wife. Nowadays men who are victimized in that manner may get involved with other women.

Third, if sexually transmitted diseases infect the husband, the wife may suggest but not demand the use of protective measures such as condoms. In fact, there have been cases where some HIV/AIDS infected men have refused to use condoms when being intimate with their uninfected wives, and that has challenged the endeavor to eradicate the pandemic. The relatives of the wife cannot intervene on behalf of their daughter because they know that the decision to have safe or unprotected sex belongs to the couple only. An infected husband who demands unsafe sexual intercourse from his uninfected wife, with the full knowledge that the wife might get the infection as well, is subjecting that woman to psychological torture.

Finally, the husband can have extramarital affairs or may marry other women, and the wife cannot challenge the husband to stop that because she has not paid for exclusive sexual rights over him. Of course, Shona men are expected to satisfy their wives sexually, but they can still be intimate with other women. Polygynous marriages bring a lot of quarrels and fighting between the woman and the husband, and also the wives themselves.

### Rights over Wife's Productive Capacity

The payment of *rugaba* also gives the husband inalienable rights over the productive capacity of his wife. Whatever she toils for, equally belongs to the man. In the past, only men legally owned the land and most of its produce. Of course, the wife was allowed to own insignificant crops such as groundnuts, sweet potatoes, and round nuts. If she were a potter, she also could keep whatever she obtained from the sale of her clay pots. In 1890, when the British introduced gainful employment in Zimbabwe, only men were expected to look for work while women stayed at home taking care of children and tilling the land.

Initially, only a few unmarried women joined men in the mines and farms as employees. Eventually, married women could also work in industries and other professions, but at the discretion of their husbands. In most cases, Shona men allowed their wives to work if they were working white collar jobs, such as nursing and teaching. The heavy industry was the preserve of men. After paying bridewealth Shona men gain the right to forbid their wives to get employment, especially if the husband gets enough money to support the family. If the wife is allowed to work, the salary that the working woman earns technically belongs to the man. Some men may allow the wife to use some of her money to cater for the household needs, but she cannot just use it in any way that is not approved by the husband.

There are many challenges that come with that. First, some talented and competent women who aspire to get gainful employment might be prevented from doing so by their husbands. If that happens, it deprives the country of making use of the talent and expertise of that particular woman. The same woman loses the opportunity to develop her skills and by so doing enhancing her self-esteem. Besides that, the wife might end up taking a profession that is approved by her husband even if she does not like it.

Second, women who are prevented from taking up gainful employment rely on their husbands' salaries for sustenance, entirely. In most cases, the husband's salary might not be sufficient to cater for all the family's needs. Such women are vulnerable to abuse because financial dependence prevents them from running away from the husband if he abuses them. Even in circumstances where the husband's salary is adequate to support the family, it just feels right for the wife to be able to contribute to the family's well-being monetarily.

Third, a working woman might be reduced to a beggar since she may not keep and use her husband's money as she likes. She may be required to seek permission from the husband to use some of the money that she earns, and some men do not readily give the requested authorization. Some of those women are accused of overspending the husband's money on trivialities. There are times when a woman thinks of assisting her relatives, but she might not be able to do that without the explicit permission of the husband. Moreover, some needs are too personal to be discussed, and, as a result, some women suffer in silence.

Fourth, even where both the wife and husband work, some men may use the money that they earn for the pursuit of pleasure while demanding that the wife uses all her money to support the family. I know of men who go to town and come back carrying their briefcases and newspapers only. They expect the wives to use all their money to buy food and clothes for the family. There are also men who squander the wife's earnings with other women without the consent of the wife.

Finally, the attainment of the above right by Shona men has led to the commercialization of bridewealth. Relatives tend to charge more bridewealth for educated women. In fact, some parents ask for a refund of their daughter's educational expenses during the bridewealth negotiations, and some people think that they are greedy. They might not be greedy at all, but they realize that once their daughter is married then, they cannot be compensated for the cattle or money that they would have spent in educating her since her salary would now belong to the husband. But charging for the daughter's educational expenses has its adverse impact on the financial assistance that they might require from their daughter in the future. Most people know that it is the responsibility of every parent to educate her or his children. Now, by asking the son-in-law to shoulder the pre-marital educational responsibilities of his wife is tantamount to making him both the father and the husband of his wife. The parents might get a refund for their daughter's educational expenses or may charge an exorbitant bridewealth to cater for their educational expenses on their daughter, but it places the daughter in a tight corner. In the future, the husband might not allow her to assist them and other relatives financially because they might have gotten their share as bridewealth already.

## Disciplining by Moderate Beating

The payment of *rugaba* also awards men the right to punish their wives by moderate beating if they fail to provide the services for which the man would have paid. This right is never communicated to the husband's delegation during and after the bridewealth negotiations, but it is assumed. There is no bridewealth portion that specifically caters for that but families that are involved in bridewealth negotiations know about it. Sometimes female relatives of the wife forewarn her about fights and quarrels that characterize many marriages and encourage her not to run away from her husband, but to bear them stoically. It should be noted that almost everyone condemns any severe beating of the wife. What Elizabeth N. Colson, who studied the Tonga of Zambia in the 1940s and 1950s, observed about the Tonga people is equally valid about the Shona. She writes that although moderate beating of one's wife is allowed among the Tonga, "there are recognized limits that the husband should not exceed. Thus, he should not beat his wife with a stick; nor may he beat her when she is naked."[28]

Holleman points out that there was wife beating among the Shona of Chikomba District where he conducted his research, although some limits were established. According to him, "A husband may beat his wife moderately when the occasion—neglect of household duties, disobedience or insubordination—warrants it . . . But on no account should it be imagined that a woman is expected to subject herself to the arbitrary whims and wishes of her husband. Women are never regarded as "property" or "chattel"; the very nature of the marriage agreement and the relations between the families-in-law sufficiently safeguard their personal integrity."[29]

So, excessive physical disciplining of the wife by her husband is regarded as abnormal by most Shona people. The husband is always answerable to his father, mother, brothers or his cattle-linked sister who would have provided bridewealth for his wife. Other members of the lineage can also intervene on behalf of the woman. In the past, wanton and severe beatings of the wife would warrant a divorce in which the wife's parents might not be required to refund all the bridewealth. It seems that since the husband would not get more cattle from his parents or sister to pay for another wife's bridewealth, many men would not want to lose their wives because of such causes.

The primary problem with this right is that the husband only acquires it, not the wife. The woman is not expected to beat up her husband, even if she has the strength and opportunity to do so. Although it is not uncommon for a woman to beat up her husband, it is a despicable disgrace and shameful humiliation to the husband's family for that to happen. Usually, Shona men

28. Colson, *Marriage and the Family among the Tonga,* 143.
29. Holleman, 208.

who are beaten by their wives are believed to have been bewitched by their wives by the way of some love potion.

Second, beating is intended to hurt the victim whether it is moderate or severe. In fact, no scale can measure the moderateness of beating one's wife. What is considered by one man to be moderate can be regarded as severe by another man. After all, beating is intended to subjugate, dehumanize, humiliate, and hurt the victim. It lowers the self-esteem of the victim because some men beat up their wives publicly. Beating causes so much fear in the victim that she ends up doing things for the husband that she would not do if she were not afraid.

The other problem with the implicit right to discipline one's wife by moderate beating is that the beating can go unreported and unchallenged because it is considered trivial and, therefore, should be ignored by the victim. A woman who reports to her parents that her husband slapped her is likely to be advised to endure it and not to report the case to the police. Some people only act when the beating becomes severe, but the perpetrator would have developed a habit that would be hard to break.

In the past, although a married woman continued to belong to her natal family, it was hard for her to get their support if she were moderately abused by her husband. According to Elizabeth Schmidt, it was not practical for a physically abused woman to get the "protection and intervention of her father and brothers" because their predominant interest was in salvaging the marriage lest they would be required to return part of the bridewealth, which in most cases, would have been spent.[30]

## Paternal Rights

The bridewealth portion that gives the husband paternal rights over the children is called *danga* (cattle). These paternal rights are acquired as soon as the husband pays a portion of *danga* or promises to pay part of it. Usually, men pay a small portion of *danga* on the day on which they pay *rugaba* so that they can gain paternal rights immediately. Once that is done, then, the children that are born by his wife belong to him and his clan. In the event of a divorce, the children are expected to remain with their father. If some of them, ordinarily the young ones, accompany their mother back to her people, they are supposed to come back to the father when they no longer rely on their mother for sustenance. The children take their father's last name and his totem. If a married woman bears a child as a result of an extramarital affair, that child belongs to the legitimate husband. The Shona

---

30. Schmidt, *Peasants, Traders, and Wives*, 21.

have a saying that goes; *gomba harina mwana* (an illicit lover has no paternal rights). He does not have paternal rights because he has not paid for them. The compensation that such a man pays to the husband of his illicit lover compensates the husband for the unlawful use of the sexual organs for which only the legal husband should have exclusive usage. A man cannot claim paternal rights over a child that he fathers with a married woman because those rights have been paid for by the legal husband. However, the formal husband may decide to forfeit his paternal rights over a child that his wife bears with an illicit lover.

Among the Shona, the acquisition of paternal rights is crucial. Suppose a married man or woman dies prematurely, before a sufficient number of children are born, a relative should replace the deceased spouse. If a wife dies before bearing an adequate number of children, a sororate marriage might be established, and if the husband dies, prematurely a levirate marriage is put in place.[31] In the past, if a married man was sterile, his brother was asked to beget children for him with his brother's wife, secretly. Of course, such an affair was not intended to be romantic, but a fulfillment of one's sacred duty. The relatives of a barren wife were expected to provide their son-in-law with another woman, preferably the wife's sister, cousin or niece.

There are many challenges that are associated with the payment of *danga*. One of the challenges that come as a result of the acquisition of paternal rights by the husband is the disenfranchisement of the wife. Her children are not quite hers because they belong to the man. She is expected to take care of them, but she knows that they belong to their father and his relatives. In the event of a divorce, she may be asked to leave behind all her children. If some of them accompany her to her parents' home, she is aware that the final say about their future lies with the husband. In their mother's home, her children are considered aliens or *vatogwa* and are expected to go back to their father's people. There are instances when modern courts of law award the custody of children to their mother, but still, everyone knows that they belong to their father. If one of the children who would have accompanied the mother to her people at divorce gets married, the son-in-law's delegation is directed to the daughter's father. However, in cases where

---

31. In a sororate marriage a man with a deceased wife was given another wife by his in-laws, usually the young sister of the deceased wife to complete the duties of the deceased woman especially that of bearing children. If the husband died a levirate marriage was put in place where a young brother of the dead man took over the social, economic, and conjugal responsibilities his brother was supposed to fulfill. Among the Shona the woman was allowed to choose one from a number of her husband's brothers. The children born out of this union belonged to his deceased brother.

*danga* was not paid in full, the relatives of a divorced woman may accept bridewealth for one of their daughter's girls to set off the balance that was not paid for their daughter.

The other challenge that the acquisition of paternal rights brings is that the wife cannot make decisions in matters concerning family planning because her child-bearing capacity has been "purchased" by her husband. If the man still wants more children, the wife must fulfill her obligation of bearing more children. Under no circumstances may a married woman decide to embark on a family planning program without the explicit permission of her husband. Again, a married woman should not fall pregnant unless the man is aware and permits it. Some women have been beaten up for becoming pregnant without first obtaining the express permission from their husbands. It is painful to know that one has no control over her reproductive capacity.

Furthermore, some abused women remain in abusive marriages because they do not want to leave their children with the abuser. Since the children belong to the husband, the mother should stay in her husband's home if she wants to take care of her children. If a divorced woman takes the children to her people after divorce, she becomes accountable for whatever happens to any of the children. If any of the girls gets married, the mother should direct the son-in-law to her ex-husband to pay bridewealth. Boys are expected to run away from their mother to live with their father. In fact, it is an enormous embarrassment, particularly for male children to live among their mother's people, if they can avoid it.

Finally, even where there is no divorce, the husband gets a lion's share of the bridewealth. In fact, the mother of the bride only gets the beast of motherhood and other insignificant payments, but the father gets almost everything. Although the father of the bride uses his lion's share of the bridewealth to support the whole family, the bride's mother may only benefit from her own daughter's bridewealth if she remains in her marital home. In the past, if she divorced or was divorced by her husband, she was expected to take with her the beast of motherhood, its offspring, and her kitchen utensils only. Although modern laws of Zimbabwe demand that the husband and wife divide their property equally between them when they divorce, some men still find ways of manipulating and exploiting their ex-wives.

## Inheritance Rights

The *danga* also gives the male relatives of the man the right to inherit the widow if the husband dies before satisfactory services would have been rendered. At least six months after the death of a married man or woman the cleansing ceremony is performed. This ceremony brings back the spirit of the dead person into the home as an ancestor. Ancestors have several responsibilities one of which is to protect the family from ubiquitous evil spirits and misfortunes. At the end of such a ritual, the estate of the dead man has to be shared among those deserving members of the extended family. The widow is also granted the opportunity to choose one of the brothers, cousins, and nephews of her dead husband to inherit her as a wife. A woman can select one of her sons to be her official guardian. If she does that, then she is expected to remain celibate and chaste as long as she lives in the home of her dead husband. In the past, the relatives of the dead man had the right to expel a woman from her deceased husband's home if she refused to be inherited but failed to lead a chaste life. Sometimes, such a woman's father would be asked to return part of the bridewealth.

The inheritance of the wife portrays her as part of her husband's estate. It also takes away the woman's freedom to choose another man after the death of her first husband without the fear of being harassed by the relatives of her late husband or his spirit. Lastly, a woman who refuses to be inherited, but then gets involved with strangers, sexually, might be alienated from her children. Some male children find it easy to accept a relative of their late father as their mother's new husband but might find it extremely hard to accept a stranger. Consequently, some women have to comply with the tradition so as to stick with their children.

## Refundability of Bridewealth

Although the refundability of bridewealth is not one of the rights that men acquire, it is an aspect of it that helps some of them to subjugate, exploit, and oppress their wives. Bridewealth is only refundable if the woman causes a divorce before a sufficient number of children are born. In the past, the adequate number of children could be eight children or even more. According to Jack Goody, if an abused woman ran away from her husband, the returnability of bridewealth pressured the woman's kin to persuade her to "rejoin her husband or enter into a new marriage."[32]

---

32. Goody and Tambiah, *Bridewealth and Dowry*, 12.

Nowadays, Shona families are becoming smaller, so, even two kids can be considered enough. In the past, not all the bridewealth would be returned to the son-in-law, but very few families were willing to do so. Usually, divorce happened when the father-in-law had already used the bridewealth, and could no longer return some of it to the son-in-law. Nowadays, very few men try to have their bridewealth refunded, and very few are successful. Be that as it may, women still know that bridewealth is refundable. So, an abused woman might put up with her abuse, fearing that her father or relatives might not be able to refund the bridewealth.

## Comments

Although bridewealth was not perfect right from its beginning, the monetization of the economy by the British made it worse. Instead of getting bridewealth from their parents or sisters, young men could now pay their bridewealth using their salaries. Consequently, bridewealth became privatized, and each man could treat his wife the way that pleased him. Since they pay, their own bridewealth, men are no longer answerable to anyone for the manner in which they treat their women. In the past, the father or sister from whom the bridewealth would have come had the right to put the husband to task if he ill-treated his wife. Furthermore, the exorbitant bridewealth that is charged frustrates and impoverishes the newlyweds before they start living together. There are instances when some girls cry and plead with their relatives to lower the bridewealth during bridewealth negotiations, although their pleading is considered improper.

Domestic violence and gender inequality are evil, and any cultural practice that tends to promote them should be challenged or transformed. Commercialization and privatization of bridewealth bring more misery to women than good. In fact, it is a dangerous myth to argue that bridewealth adds value to women because it in fact reduces their value. The more the bridewealth that is paid for a particular woman, the greater her marital responsibilities, and perhaps her subjugation and exploitation by her husband. Women, just like men, were created in the image of God, and by that, they have the same value as men. There is no amount of money or cows that can increase the value of women. Perhaps the question to ask at this point is; if bridewealth were to be abolished today, who stands to lose between men and women? Yes, it is our cultural heritage, but unless some laws regulate it, then it is open to abuse by unscrupulous parents.

Can there ever be a complete emancipation of Shona women? Never; as long as bridewealth exists in the manner it does today. Shona women cannot have both bridewealth paid for them and total freedom. Without the abolishment or regulation of bridewealth, the cry for the complete emancipation of Shona women remains a wild goose chase. Aeneas S. Chigwedere argues that reform is better than abolishment.[33] Whatever, the future of bridewealth would be, for now, it is a wolf that is clothed in sheep's skin. It is a poison that has been wrapped in Christmas wrappers. Is it part of the Shona culture? Yes, it is, but who says that culture is static and does not need any transformation?

33. Chigwedere, *Lobola*, 56.

# Chapter 4

## Religious Tradition on Marriage and Women

### Introduction

CHAPTER 4 DEALS WITH the religious tradition regarding the position of women, marriage, and domestic violence, particularly, in the Roman Catholic Church. This chapter attends to the many positive things that the Roman Catholic Church teaches about women and marriage, but also revisits some of the unfavorable teachings on women and marriage that may have contributed to the suppression of women both in the church and society. The predominant purpose of this chapter is to provide a brief but pertinent exploration of how the Roman Catholic Church has viewed and interacted with women, right from the beginning of Christianity up to the present day. This information is important because it allows us to discern the kind of resources that are available in the Catholic tradition concerning the emancipation of women in the world, particularly in Zimbabwe, that theologians can tap into. It should be noted that some of those resources might have been used to promote patriarchy at the expense of the equality between women and men.

This chapter has five sections, and each section has three parts. Section 1 deals with Jesus' attitude towards and interaction with women according to the Gospel of Luke. Section 2 evaluates how the Apostle Paul viewed women and marriage in some of his letters. Section 3 deals with one of the greatest church fathers, Tertullian's teachings on women and marriage. Section 4 explores Pope John Paul II's thoughts on women, marriage, and domestic violence. Lastly, section 5 assesses the Zimbabwe Catholic Bishops'

Conference on women, family, and violence. The first part of each section explains the positive teachings and views on marriage and women. In most cases, these are teachings that seek to enhance the dignity of human beings as creatures created in the image of God, irrespective of their gender. The second part of each section looks at the negative attitudes and teachings that can be interpreted as presenting women as inferior to men, and married life as inferior to celibacy. The third part of each section offers some analysis of each section.

## Jesus' Attitude toward Women according to the Gospel of Luke

The Roman Catholic Church traces its origins back to Jesus Christ, who most people of his time knew as the son of Mary and Joseph, although his followers believed that he was the Son of God. He was born in 4 BC, in Bethlehem of Judaea, and grew up in Nazareth in Galilee. At the age of thirty, he became a renowned preacher and miracle worker, and challenged the religious status quo of his time, which led to his condemnation and death on the cross at the hands of the Romans and some Jewish leaders. Jesus' exact year of birth is controversial among biblical scholars, but many agree that he was born between 4 BCE and 6 BCE.[1] Although there is no record of his educational background, he was one of the greatest teachers of his time who utilized parables as a teaching methodology. Most New Testament scholars concur that the reign of God was at the center of his message. He also performed miracles to the greatest amazement and admiration of his followers. His teachings and deeds created enemies among the most influential political and religious leaders of his society. He died on the cross, and many biblical scholars contend that his death came as a result of his constant process of upsetting the status quo by what could be considered radical and revolutionary teachings, especially through his association with the marginalized people of his time.[2] Thus, Norman Perrin remarks, "Jesus welcomed . . . outcasts into table-fellowship with himself in the name of the kingdom of God, in the name of the Jews' ultimate hope, and so both prostituted that hope and shattered the closed ranks of the community against their enemy. It is hard to image anything more offensive to Jewish sensibilities."[3]

In the Jewish society where he was born, women were among the marginalized groups of people. Although the Jewish society of that time

1. Grant, *Jesus: An Historian's Review of the Gospels*, 71.
2. Freyne, *Galilee, Jesus and the Gospels*, 54.
3. Perrin, *Rediscovering the Teachings of Jesus*, 103.

respected women as mothers and occasionally, as spiritual leaders, some of them considered women to be inferior to men due to their subjection to "multiple legal impurities" such as menstruation.[4] According to Elizabeth Schussler Fiorenza, in Judaism, males were seen as religiously and socially privileged.[5] Jesus shocked his contemporaries by his positive attitude towards women that some New Testament scholars say was without parallel in the Jewish history.[6]

Jesus' association with women tells us more about his positive attitude towards them. According to the Gospel of Luke, several women associated with Jesus and assisted him in many different ways. Of the four canonical Gospels, the Gospel of Luke has the largest number of stories which involve women. Luke has forty-two passages about women of which twenty-three are unique to him. Ten women are mentioned by name as compared to one hundred and thirty-three men.[7] Some of those mentioned by name are Mary, the mother of Jesus, Mary Magdalene, Mary, the mother of James, Joanna, the wife of Chuza, Salome, Elizabeth, Anna, and Mary and Martha of Bethany. There are other women whose names are not mentioned, but Jesus associated with them in one way or another. For instance, Simon's mother-in-law, (4:39), the widow of Nain (7:11–17), the woman who was stooped (13:10–17), and others.

Many New Testament scholars have analyzed the Gospel of Luke to discern Jesus' attitude towards the women of his time. Barbara E. Reid has suggested that to discover Jesus' attitude towards women we ought to first define discipleship. The question is: did women participate in the mission of Jesus in the same way that the male disciples did?[8] She identifies the marks of discipleship as being that of hearing (Luke 4:15), seeing (Luke 23:47), and obeying the word of God.[9] She defines a disciple as one who "participates in the mission of Jesus by doing what he did: preaching, teaching, healing, exorcising, forgiving, serving, and enduring conflicts and persecutions."[10] This definition of discipleship will help us to evaluate Jesus' attitude towards the women of his time. It appears that Jesus allowed women to be his disciples and to accompany him with the apostles as he journeyed through

4. Gryson, *The Ministry of Women in the Early Church*, 1.

5. Schüssler Fiorenza, *In Memory of Her*, 218.

6. Meskeen, *Women*, 10–11.

7. Schaberg, "Luke," 279–80.

8. Reid, *Choosing the Better Half?*, 3.

9. Ibid., 22.

10. Ibid., 24.

cities and villages.[11] Of all the women named above, Luke mentions Mary, the mother of Jesus thirteen times.[12] Mary is honored by many Christian traditions for having given her consent to be the mother of Jesus and as a model of authentic discipleship.[13]

According to Jane Schaberg, the Gospel of Luke seems to suggest a vibrant discipleship of women by using the technique which is called "pairing." She says that most of the parables in which men are mentioned have a parallel parable in which there is a woman. The same is said to apply to healing incidents as well. She gives examples of the parable of the Lost Sheep that is followed by the parable of the Lost Coin (15:4–10), the healing of the widow's son (7:17) that is followed by the healing of Jairus' daughter (8:42), and other examples.[14] That pairing seems to suggest that women in the Gospel of Luke were treated as equals to men in issues concerning discipleship. It also appears to suggest that Jesus would not act differently with men than he would with women and by so doing, he was emphasizing the equality between women and men.

Several biblical scholars have supported the notion that the Lukan Jesus treated women with care, concern, respect, and dignity. Jesus showed great concern for them by curing them of a variety of ailments. Jesus' honor and respect for women were not reserved only for his mother, but it was also extended to all women. He publicly showed his concern for the woman that he healed on the Sabbath and called her a "daughter of Abraham" (Luke 13:10–13). That statement should have restored her dignity that she had lost because of her illness.

In the Gospel of Luke, women were also commissioned to announce the Good News of the proximity and arrival of the realm of God. In addition to that, some women from Galilee were the first to witness the remarkable and incredible news of the resurrection of the Lord and that "confirmed their discipleship" since they were trustworthy and credible witnesses.[15] One striking example of such a reliable and authoritative woman was Mary Magdalene, who Turid Karlsen Seim calls "an authority comparable to Peter on the male side."[16] Wherever women are mentioned in the Gospel of Luke, Mary Magdalene is mentioned first, and some biblical scholars have attributed that to her leadership qualities. Thus, Michael Grant remarks, "As every

---

11. Gryson, *The Ministry of Women in the Early Church*, 2.

12. Fitzmyer, *Luke the Theologian*, 57.

13. Obach and Kirk, *A Commentary on the Gospel of Luke*, 20.

14. Schaberg, "Luke," 278.

15. Seim, "The Gospel of Luke," 749–50.

16. Ibid., 735.

Gospel agrees, Jesus' female followers remained conspicuously faithful to him right up to and after his death, exceeding in loyalty and understanding not only the single apostle Judas who betrayed him but all the other apostles as well, including Peter who was said to have denied him three times."[17]

Jesus respected women's rights to life and free association. He allowed the women that he healed from various sicknesses to follow him if they chose to do so or to go home to their families. Although women did not claim to have rights, Jesus acknowledged that they had rights, and he healed them.[18] He also allowed them to touch him, and he forgave them their sins (Luke 7:37). Brennan Hill, remarks that in the story of the woman who came to Jesus at the house of Simon the Pharisee (Luke 7:36–50) and in others, Jesus set aside the taboos that "decreed that he could not touch or be touched by women or speak to them in public. With courage and openness, he reaches out to women who are marginal, diseased, even disgraced, and offers them freedom and wholeness."[19] In the Jewish society of that period, some illnesses were thought to be a result of one's sins and when Jesus forgave these women their sins, he wanted to set them free from the stigma that their illness had on their personal dignity.

The above examples show us that Jesus treated women with respect, concern, care, and gave them the dignity that was fitting for human beings created in the image of God. That attitude shows that Jesus did not have the same concern over gender differences between women and men that some of his contemporaries had.

But, was Jesus' treatment of women sufficient to sow and cultivate the spirit of equality among Christians? Some feminist theologians argue that although the Lukan Jesus treated women with dignity, women's ministerial roles were played down. Barbara E. Reid says that "although it is indisputable that there are women disciples in Luke and Acts, a closer study reveals that they do not participate in the mission of Jesus in the same way that men disciples do."[20] There is no equality between men and women in this discipleship. There are no individual women being "called, commissioned, enduring persecution, or ministering by the power of the Holy Spirit."[21] Barbara Reid goes on to argue that although Elizabeth, Mary the mother of Jesus, and Anna were powerful women among the disciples of Jesus, they belonged to an era of Judaism and as such they were not disciples of Jesus in

17. Grant, *Jesus: An Historian's Review of the Gospels*, 85.

18. Seim, "The Gospel of Luke," 739.

19. Hill, *Jesus the Christ: Contemporary Perspectives*, 109.

20. Reid, *Choosing the Better Half?*, 3.

21. Ibid., 52.

the strict sense of the word. The other Lukan women did not imitate Jesus' mission of preaching, healing, exorcising, teaching, praying or forgiving as the male followers did. Women were, in fact, passive recipients of Jesus' compassion and healing.[22] Whenever the women tried to speak, they were reprimanded by Jesus and disbelieved, and their service was ancillary to that of the male disciples.[23]

John Duns Scotus (d. 1308) is said to have argued that the legend of Mary Magdalene should not be taken as the norm because she was an individual woman who happened to enjoy a personal privilege given to her by Jesus that did not apply to other women in general.[24] Although Mary of Bethany is praised for listening to Jesus, she remained passive, and her actions are not known.

Feminist theologians agree that the Lukan women are silenced and have passive roles although Jesus respected them. Some women biblical scholars, such as Teresa Okure argue that women's contributions were either left out or downplayed in the New Testament writings.[25] This downplaying and omission had the effect of belittling or rendering invisible women's work and discipleship. Jane Schaberg accuses Luke of having "blurred" the traditional and historical part of women's leadership to the advantage of men's leadership.[26] According to Schussler Fiorenza, although Jesus sympathized with the marginalized that included women, he did not explicitly articulate a systematic strategy for structural change.[27]

Despite the Lukan Jesus' seemingly unequal attitude towards women as compared to his attitude towards men, feminist theologians agree that there could have been more women followers of Jesus than those that are mentioned in Luke, and their active participation could have been downplayed by Luke, not by Jesus. Although we can only know Jesus' attitude towards women through what is written by the gospel writers, their reporting of the stories about women cannot always be an infallible guide to the actions and attitude of Jesus. There is enough evidence for us to infer that Jesus treated women with respect and dignity. Even the few stories about women in the Gospel of Luke tell us more about Jesus' positive attitude about women. What is needed is the unmasking of the stories' patriarchal framework as Barbara Reid has pointed out. The few stories about women

22. Ibid.

23. Ibid.

24. Cooke and Macy, *A History of Women and Ordination*, 81.

25. Okure, "Contemporary Perspectives on Women in the Bible," 8.

26. Schaberg, "Luke," 279.

27. Schüssler Fiorenza, *In Memory of Her*, 142.

that we find in Luke should "confront us with the reliability, giftedness, and resources of women for mission and invite us to reevaluate any restrictions of access to ministry on the basis of gender alone."[28]

Nowhere in the Gospel of Luke does Jesus speak ill of women. According to Brennan Hill, "there is no evidence that he talked down to women, considered them to be inferior, seductive, or in any way less worthy of human rights and freedom than men."[29] If he had a negative attitude towards women, he could have said it in public. On the contrary, he showed compassion on them and treated them with the dignity that human beings deserved, irrespective of their gender. Elizabeth Schussler Fiorenza writes about the vision of Jesus concerning women as a *basileia* vision of Jesus that summoned women from poverty and ostracization to wholeness and selfhood.[30]

In the Gospel of Luke Jesus did not explicitly tackle the question of domestic violence and marriage. One of the reasons for the omissions may be that domestic violence was not one of the topical issues during his ministry. However, Jesus' positive attitude towards women emphasized women's dignity, liberty, respect, and equality with men. If Jesus gave women the same dignity, respect and freedom as that granted to men, it follows then that Jesus would be against anything that would disturb that dignity, respect, and freedom. Domestic violence, particularly wife battering undermines all of the above. One can imagine a situation where a battered woman, would be brought to Jesus for his counsel. It is hard to imagine Jesus condemning such a woman for being battered. He did not condemn the woman who was caught committing adultery and was brought to him.

## Paul on Women and Marriage

The Apostle Paul is the most prolific author and apostle of the early Christian era. He wrote many letters to Christian communities most of which he had founded. When it comes to his thinking about women, there are several divergent opinions. Some see Paul as one who hated women and encouraged the perpetuation of their inferiority. This view is based on the argument that since Paul had grown up in a chauvinistic society and had trained to be a rabbi under Gamaliel, it could have been natural for him to consider women as inferior to men[31] Other biblical scholars disagree with this allegation, and

---

28. Reid, *Choosing the Better Half?*, 207.

29. Hill, *Jesus the Christ: Contemporary Perspectives*, 108.

30. Schüssler Fiorenza, *In Memory of Her*, 154.

31. House, "Paul, Women, and Contemporary Evangelical Feminism," 40

they, in fact, argue that Paul loved and respected women, and treated them as equals in his missionary work.[32] Another school of thought argues that Paul was undecided about the women of his time and his attitude was both positive and negative.

Those who support that Paul loved and respected women provide a list of names of women who were associated with Paul and argue that if Paul hated women, he could have avoided associating with them. Some of the women who knew Paul were, Lois and Eunice (2 Timothy 1:5), Damaris (Acts 17:34), Lydia (Acts 16:11–40), Chloe (1 Corinthians 1:11), Euodia (Phil 4:2–3), Priscilla (1 Corinthians 16:19), Phoebe (Romans 16:1–2), and others.[33] Paul worked in ministry with some of these women. Gail R. O'Day thinks that Paul gave Priscilla and Aquila the responsibility for the mission at Ephesus where the two instructed Apollos in the Good News of Jesus. According to her, Priscilla and other women were indispensable to Paul's ministry.[34] Richard and Joyce Boldrey describe Priscilla as someone who was respected and "highly regarded by Paul."[35]

According to Luke, women were among Paul's first converts (Acts 16:14) and at times, they provided shelter to Paul and other ministers (Acts 16:40). Some of those women prophesied in worship assemblies, for example, the daughters of Philip.[36] So, one could argue that Paul respected women and considered them fellow-workers in his missionary journeys.

In support of the above sentiments, some New Testament scholars argue that Paul's positive attitude towards women can be found in his letter to the Galatians, especially, chapter 3:28 that says that there was to be no difference between women and men who believed in Christ. H. W. House considers Galatians 3:28 as a breakthrough in the proper attitude toward women by Paul. For him, "Galatians 3:28 is a theological statement directed against what is called the order of creation, and it creates a tension with those biblical passages used to subordinate women."[37] H. W. House argues that Galatians 3:28, sums up the "emancipation theology" that consummated Jesus' attitude towards women.[38]

However, some scholars have argued that Galatians 3:28 was not composed by Paul, but was borrowed from a famous baptismal hymn of

32. Ibid., 41.

33. Gillman, Women Who Knew Paul, 23–49.

34. O'Day, "Acts," 311.

35. Boldrey, Chauvinist or Feminist?, 20.

36. McGrath, Women and the Church, 40.

37. House, "Paul, Women, and Contemporary Evangelical Feminism," 43.

38. Ibid.

that time. Elizabeth S. Fiorenza argues that, even if Paul was quoting the baptismal hymn, there are several Pauline additions in the hymn. According to her, the words "therefore" and "through the faith in Christ Jesus" and Galatians 3:29 seem to have been added to the hymn by Paul himself.[39] At baptism, it was believed that women became equal with men and also that baptism gave them the authority to teach and preach.[40] According to Brendan Byrne, what Paul says in Galatians 3:28 was not unique to the Christian community, but it was an expression of the longing for "unification and equality that were pervasive throughout the world at that time."[41]

It does not matter whether the idea of equality was not unique to the early Christian communities or Paul, but the fact that Paul quoted the verse showed that he supported the equality of men and women. The Galatian women who read the verse should have rejoiced because it intended to emancipate them from male subordination. The verse could also have ignited a theological discernment concerning the position of women in the early church.

The equality about which Paul wrote to the Galatians was demonstrated in the way he dealt with the marriage question at Corinth. The issue of marriage and conjugal rights seemed to have become a problem during Paul's time. In 1 Corinthians 7: 1–16, he addressed that issue. Paul unwaveringly affirmed the equality of married couples and the need for reciprocal fairness when it came to the fulfillment of their conjugal rights. It seems that there is nothing that Paul says in this passage that could have misled people into believing that women were inferior to men and that sexual intercourse was evil. Although he wished that Christians were celibate like himself, Paul maintained that both marriage and freedom from the marriage were callings and charisms from God.[42]

Although Paul respected women and considered them as equal partners in his missionary work, some biblical passages exhibit the subsequent denial of this equality between men and women. According to Rosemary Radford Ruether, elsewhere, Paul taught something that could be interpreted to mean that women were inferior to men. This negative teaching about women is a contradiction that explains why women's issues continued to be

39. Schüssler Fiorenza, *In Memory of Her*, 208.

40. Ruether, "St. Paul, Friend or Enemy of Women?," http://www.saintjohnorthodox.org/Saint%20Paul%20&%20Women.pdf (accessed on August 11, 2016).

41. Byrne, *Paul and the Christian Woman*, 7.

42. Schüssler Fiorenza, *In Memory of Her*, 223.

discussed by the early Christians and was modified to suit the patriarchal predominance of the society in which these debates took place.[43]

Paul has been found wanting in the same passage where he confirmed the equality and mutuality of conjugal rights between Christian couples. According to Fiorenza, the rights that Paul wrote about were merely marital and had nothing to do with the social rights of women. She goes on to say that Paul's reference to celibacy as better than married life implicitly limited married women to the confinements of the patriarchal family and "disqualified married people theologically as less engaged missionaries and less dedicated Christians."[44] What he wrote could have created a division between married women and the unmarried virgins.

Paul has also been found wanting in other passages as far as the equality of women and men, and women's dignity are concerned. One of the Pauline passages that have been analyzed in connection with Paul's negative attitude towards women is 1 Corinthians 11:1–16. In this passage, Paul tells women to cover their heads during worship, and he gave the order of creation as a reason for that. Paul outlines a hierarchical structure in which God is the head of Christ, Christ being the head of a man, and the man being the head of the woman, and because of that the woman was supposed to cover her head as a sign of her respect of her "head," —the man.

Here, Paul seems to contradict himself, particularly, his preaching of equality between men and women in Galatians 3:28. If Paul were convinced that the baptism that Christians had received had transformed them into a new creation that was not bound by gender, social, and racial divisions, then, it would not be justified to tell women to cover their heads in the church. According to Brendan Byrne, Paul seems to move away from and undermines the liberating and enlightened stress on mutuality and equality found in Galatians 3:28 and 1 Corinthians 7, and for Byrne, it "is unforgivable."[45]

Many explanations have been given for the above paradigm shift by Paul. Craig S. Keener has admitted that the passage is authentically Pauline, but the head coverings were intended for a particular cultural situation to prevent the conservative women from being scandalized by the more liberated ones at Corinth.[46] He concluded that Paul was writing to the Corinthian women, and his arguments for the head covering were not intended

43. Ibid., 3.

44. Ibid., 224, 226.

45. Byrne, *Paul and the Christian Woman*, 31.

46. Keener, "Was Paul for or Against Women in Ministry?," http://enrichmentjournal.ag.org/200102/082_paul.cfm (accessed on January 20, 2008).

to be implemented transculturally.[47] Craig S. Keener thinks that Paul was trying to impress Rome by showing that Christianity was in compliance with Jewish cultural expectations of women. In agreement with Keener, Sister Albertus M. McGrath says that Paul was trying to find a balance between the "Libertines" and "Puritanical zealots," and that he was addressing a specific issue at a particular place and time which was not intended to be universally binding.[48]

Other biblical scholars have argued that since the passage is contradictory to Paul's message of equality in Galatians 3:28, then the passage is not authentically Pauline, but an insertion of someone who wanted to oppress women.[49] Roger Gryson thinks that the solution to the contradiction is simple. He argues that 1 Corinthians 11 and 14: 34–35 "are an interpolation which have nothing to do with the genuine text of chapter 14 or Paul's true thought," and these verses were probably added by some ancient writer.[50] According to Schussler Fiorenza, here, Paul refers to loose styles of hair not veils that were negatively portrayed in Jewish circles, as unclean and a sign of moral looseness of a woman.[51]

Another passage that seems to suggest that Paul was against women is 1 Corinthians 14:34–35, where Paul directs women to be silent in church. This passage seems to contradict other passages where Paul had allowed women to prophesy in church. Some scholars argue that it was contradictory for Paul to allow women to prophesy yet commanded them to be silent in Church.[52]

Norbert Baumert argues that the passage is genuinely Pauline, and it shows that God's work of salvation is historical. It leaves a person in her or his situation to allow a gradual internal progress.[53] He goes on to say that what Jesus and Paul did was to point to new directions which were open for new developments in society and church.[54] What he is saying is that we need not criticize Jesus and Paul for their omissions regarding women emancipation because they did their share of work and the early Christians should have built on their positive attitudes. For Schussler Fiorenza, the

---

47. Keener, *Paul, Women and Wives*, 31–32.

48. McGrath, *Women and the Church*, 47.

49. See, Byrne, *Paul and the Christian Woman*, 34–51.

50. Gryson, *Ministry of Women in the Early Church*, 6–7.

51. Schüssler Fiorenza, *In Memory of Her*, 228.

52. Bassler, "1 Corinthians," 237–38.

53. Baumert, *Woman and Man in Paul*, 198.

54. Ibid., 212.

passages should be accepted as original Pauline statements that should be understood within their contexts.[55]

Some scholars have viewed Paul as a theological schizophrenic. This position is said to have been taken by evangelical feminists.[56] This school of thought argues that there is a dichotomy between Paul as a rabbi, and Paul as a Christian. As a rabbi Paul tried to be faithful to his patriarchal tradition which saw women as unequal to men. Paul as a Christian accepted the equality of men and women and tried to implement it. So, there is tension between the apostle Paul and Paul, the rabbi, and this is said to have led to contradictions in what Paul wrote about women.[57]

H. W. House has criticized this approach for discrediting the evangelical notion of inspiration. House is afraid that the above position may lead evangelicals to the rejection of Paul's authority as an apostle.[58] He then concludes that Paul's teaching and attitude about women were in line with Jesus' view of women which, according to him were more in favor of men than women.[59]

According to Brendan Byrne, whatever explanation can be given for these passages, the historical damage that they caused cannot be undone.[60] Women have been subordinated and subjugated both in society and church, partly because of these passages. While Paul can be used in the fight for women emancipation in the world and Zimbabwe, in particular, some of the passages attributed to him have been used to harm women and may continue to do so unless a liberationist interpretation of those passages is utilized. Some scholars have called for a holistic judgment of Paul's attitude towards women by considering other good things he says about women in other passages.

Paul seems to have written his letters to address particular Christian communities concerning specific issues which required his intervention. It seems that the question of anachronism was never raised as an issue that needed Paul's advice. Despite Paul's silence on domestic violence, one can infer from the dignity that he gives to women that he is not likely to have supported it. The equality between women and men, which he preached demanded that one would not do to others what he did not want to be done to him.

---

55. Schüssler Fiorenza, *In Memory of Her*, 231.

56. House, "Paul, Women, and Contemporary Evangelical Feminism," 42.

57. Ibid., 43.

58. Ibid., 46.

59. Ibid., 48–51.

60. Byrne, *Paul and the Christian Woman*, 65.

## Tertullian on Women and Marriage

Quintus Septimus Florens Tertullian (155–222 CE) was born in Carthage in the Roman province of Africa, in present-day Tunisia, to a father who was a centurion.[61] Tertullian is believed to have received an exceptional education in grammar, literature, rhetoric, law, and philosophy. After his education in Carthage, he is thought to have gone to Rome for further studies and to practice law. At a later date, perhaps around 185 CE, he converted to Christianity and started writing in defense of Christianity.[62] There are disagreements among church historians concerning the status of Tertullian in the church. Some historians argue that he was a lay man, and others say he was a priest. According to Timothy D. Barnes, "Tertullian never describes himself as ordained or appeals to his position as a priest in order to strengthen an argument," but twice he classified himself as a lay person, and it was St. Jerome who wrote that Tertullian was a priest.[63]

Many Christian historians agree that Tertullian is crucial to the discussion concerning the emancipation of women because the Western Church is greatly indebted to him for the Catholic teaching and literature. His attitude towards Christian doctrine is said to have been mixed with moral rigor and an uncompromising stand against worldly standards, a religious disposition, which led him to leave the church to join the schismatic Montanists around 207 CE.[64] However, some scholars think that although there is enough evidence that Tertullian became a Montanist, he never left Orthodoxy Christianity. To that effect, David Rankin argues that "Tertullian was no schismatic. Reports of a breach with the Catholic Church have been exaggerated. The extent of the influence of Montanism on Tertullian has also been overstated."[65] About Tertullian's moral severity, Gerald L. Bray wrote: "It is tempting to ascribe such rigorism to his temperament, or to the influence of Montanism, but the problem is not so simple. Rigidity to the point of enforced uniformity of practice, as well as belief, has always been a feature of the Western Church."[66]

Tertullian, like other Church Fathers who came after him, wrote both positive and negative things concerning women and marriage. His writings

61. Thurston, *Widows*, 77.

62. Ibid.

63. Barnes, *Tertullian*, 11, 31.

64. Thurston, *Widows*, 77–79.

65. Rankin, *Tertullian and the Church*, 3, 41.

66. Bray, *Holiness and the Will of God*, 97.

can be dated to between 195 and 220 CE.[67] For him, marriage between believers was ratified by God himself, and he marveled at the oneness, equality, and mutuality that such marriage brings to the couple.[68] Tertullian seems to suggest that Christian women could do all that Christian men could do in the Christian community. This perspective should have been a great encouragement to the women who read or heard it. It should also have encouraged men to treat their wives with dignity even outside church premises. Tertullian also supported the phenomenon of women prophecy in the church. Some "sisters" are reported to have been seeing visions during the Christian worship, and they would explain them to the people after the service.[69] Although the explanation of the vision was to be done after the service, this should have fostered a feeling of equality between men and women.

Tertullian also taught that men and women were equal by being the recipients of the "angelic nature."[70] He argued that since the soul had no a pre-established sex, women and men were equal. Furthermore, women and men were members of the same church, and they could profit from the same spiritual gifts, especially the gift of prophecy.[71] So, both men and women were equal in their endeavor to attain holiness.

In his book, *Adversus Marcionem*, Tertullian praised Mary, the mother of Jesus. According to him, if Eve was deceived by the snake, Mary through her trust of the angel Gabriel had gained life from God. Because of that, both women and men would be resurrected on the last day to enjoy everlasting life.[72] Tertullian had a high estimation of women martyrs since they could face martyrdom just like men.[73] This encouragement shows that Tertullian believed that women just as men could withstand the torture of the executioner.

A select group of widows existed in Carthage, and Tertullian wrote about them as a special group of women of sixty years and older. They were highly regarded and qualified women who had a place in the assembly.[74] Tertullian had high regard for the order of the widows who are mentioned

---

67. Quasten, *Patrology*, 247.

68 *Ad Uxorem* 2.8 (198/203CE), as cited in LaPorte, *Role of Women in Early Christianity*, 27–28. (All the dates given have been adapted from Barnes, *Tertullian*, 55.)

69. *De Anima* 9 (206/207 CE), as cited in Hoffman, *Status of Women and Gnosticism in Irenaeus and Tertullian*, 173;

70. *De Cultu Feminarum* 1.2.5 (205/206 CE); ibid., 157.

71. Ibid.

72. *Adversus Marcionem* 3.11 (207/207 CE); ibid., 158;

73. Ibid., 169.

74. *De Virginibus Velandis* 9 (208/209 CE); ibid., 163.

together with the male hierarchy of the church and ranked among the cler-
gy.[75] Only women who would have been single-husbanded, mothers and
educators of children were accepted into the order, and their main duties
included giving counsel and comfort among others.[76] According to David
Rankin, Tertullian does not mention a specific ministry of the widows but
he admits that, clearly they were part of a "well- defined and prestigious
group within the life of the Church."[77]

Despite the positive things Tertullian wrote about women, there are
other things that he wrote about women that are not helpful in the fight for
women emancipation. This paradigm shift has been attributed to his faith
change from orthodoxy to Montanism. Montanism was founded by Mon-
tanus in Asia Minor in the middle of the second century. The Montanists'
faith revolved around two main beliefs. First, they taught that the end of
the world was imminent "as evidenced by wars and rebellions," and that the
new Jerusalem was about to descend from heaven.[78] Second, they firmly
believed that marriage was an earthly bond preventing full consecration
to God, and they forbade second marriages as well as new ones.[79] Some
scholars argue that Tertullian's spiritual rigor was a result of his Montanistic
leanings.

In his book, *De Cultu Feminarum*, that was written in 205 or 206 CE,
Tertullian argues that only men, not women were the image of God. For
him, men were closer to God than women. That mentality could have led
some men to belittle women. The equality between women and men has
its basis in the fact that both women and men were created in the image of
God and to deny that fact was to destroy the foundation on which gender
equality was built.

Tertullian also blamed women for the first sin that he said extended
from Eve to all other women.[80] Most critics of Tertullian quote the following: "You are the devil's gateway: you are the unsealer of that (forbidden)
tree: you are the first deserter of the divine law: you are she who persuaded
him who the devil was not valiant enough to attack."[81] Tertullian also firmly
believed that women were the source of temptations. He condemned the

75. *De Virginibus Velandis*, as cited in Gryson, *Ministry of Women in the Early
Church*, 21.

76. Thurston, *Widows*, 81.

77. Rankin, *Tertullian and the Church*, 178.

78. Thurston, *Widows*, 78.

79. Ibid.

80. Clark, *Women in the Early Church*, 15.

81. *De Cultu Feminarum* 1.1 (205/206 CE), as cited in Young, ed., *An Anthology of
Sacred Texts by and About Women*, 8.

make-up women wore and argued that it was intended to lure men into sexual temptations. He criticized the wearing of ornaments and jewelry because he believed that those things were part of the evil world system that should be rejected by the Christians.[82]

Tertullian was against women teaching in church or baptizing as had become a habit among the heretics. He categorically stated that women were not allowed to speak in church. They were also not permitted to teach or to baptize. He criticized heretic women who were allowed to teach, speak in church, and probably to baptize. About those women, he wrote that "they all arrogantly claim knowledge, they know their catechism before they learn it. Their immodest women dare to teach and dispute, perform exorcisms, promise cures, and perhaps even baptize converts."[83] He even condemned the Acts of Paul and Thecla, which he said could influence women to claim the right to teach and baptize. Tertullian denounced the book as inauthentic because there was no way Paul could have allowed Thecla to teach and baptize since he was the one who had banned women from speaking in church.[84] Even if the above were Tertullian's personal feelings, not the official teachings of the church, they portrayed women as inferior to men. Tertullian also taught that it was better not to marry, and he condemned second marriages as a form of fornication."[85] According to Jean LaPorte, "as a Montanist by personal inclination Tertullian was an Encratist. For this reason, he condemned second marriage, and came to deny bishops the right to forgive the so-called irremissible sins."[86] By saying so, Tertullian discouraged marriage although he seemed to have supported it initially. Tertullian also imposed the wearing of veils by women. According to Bonnie B. Thurston, Tertullian did not seem to know that Paul had permitted women to pray and prophesy in public worship. He also ordered all married and virgins to be veiled.[87]

Tertullian's views about women give evidence of one of the mentality about women that dominated in the patristic period, and that has probably continued up to recent times. Men, such as Tertullian were theologians who were products of their times. They were influenced by the philosophies,

82. Hoffman, *Status of Women and Gnosticism in Irenaeus and Tertullian*, 150.

83. *De Praescriptione Haereticorum* 41.1ff, as cited in Barnes, *Tertullian*, 117.

84. *De Baptismo* 17 (198/203 CE), as cited in Gryson, *Ministry of Women in the Early Church*, 19.

85. *De Exhortatione Castitatis* 9 (208/209 CE), as cited in Clark, *Women in the Early Church*, 149.

86. LaPorte, *Role of Women in Early Christianity*, 29.

87. *De Virginibus Velandis* 5, 8, and 11 (208/209 CE), as cited in Thurston, *Widows*, 79–80.

cultures, and ideas of their times. It would be unfair to judge them using today's standards and scientific knowledge, which they did not have during Tertullian's time. Daniel L. Hoffman argues that Tertullian's view of women was generally positive.[88] Although there were compromises that Tertullian was willing to make concerning the ministry of women, there was a limit to which he wanted to go in that regard.[89]

## Pope John Paul II on Women and Marriage

The Papal office gives Popes the authority to teach and lead the people of God in matters concerning faith, morality, and society. One of the social and religious issues that have remained unresolved and in the spotlight for a long time involves the position of women in religion and society. Many Popes, just like other religious and societal leaders have explored women's place and contribution in religion and society as compared to that of men. Of all the Popes that have shown an interest in such issues, John Paul II is believed to have worked more tirelessly for the transformation of the Roman Catholic Church with an endeavor to foster equality between men and women by emphasizing the dignity and significance of women in the church and society. He stressed the dignity of all human beings, irrespective of their color, gender, race and nationality. He wrote several pastoral letters about and to women, and because of that his teachings and writings concerning women deserve a special place in any work that seeks to liberate women from male dominance.

Although Pope John Paul II wrote about and to women throughout his pontifical life, the year 1995 witnessed an intensification of his concern about women. There was a sense of urgency in his letters to resolve the problem of imbalances between women and men both in the Roman Catholic Church and the society. One of the reason could have been that he wanted to move along the signs of the time because that was the year when women, the world over, were preparing for the United Nations Women's Conference in Beijing that took place in September 1995. The other reason could be that Pope John Paul II lived at a time when these issues could no longer be ignored because of the increased gender equality consciousness in other areas of human endeavor. In January1995, Pope John Paul II published his *World Day of Peace Message* in which he dealt with women as major participants, or initiators in peacebuilding. From March to September of the same year, he published the eleven short talks that he called *The Angelus Reflections.*

88. Hoffman, *Status of Women and Gnosticism in Irenaeus and Tertullian*, 148.

89. Ibid., 177.

In September of the same year he wrote the *Letter to Women*. The central theme of his message in these letters concerned the dignity and emancipation of women from exploitative cultural practices that subordinated them to men.

In his *World Day of Peace* Message, Pope John Paul II invited women to be teachers of peace, a path that he acknowledged to having been walked by many women in the history of humankind.[90] The Pope went on to praise women in their role of rearing children and giving those children the first sense of security, and the development of their own personal identity. Due to that crucial and foundational work of women, the family becomes the first and fundamental school of social living and peace.[91] The Pope earnestly implored women to take their place in society as peace builders and encouraged them to fight against violence. He also encouraged every person of goodwill to assist women who are suffering because of bad decisions that human beings, particularly men make. He ended the message by pointing to Mary, the Mother of Jesus, as the model of peace that women may emulate.[92]

In his first Angelus Reflection titled *The Feminine Presence in the Family*, Pope John Paul II affirmed the human dignity of women as people created in the image of God. He prayed that women of the world would obtain an informed and active consciousness of their dignity, gifts, and mission.[93] He encouraged humanity to respect the equality of every man and woman in every walk of life. The Pope traced the origins of this balance to the creation story in Genesis where God created man and woman in his own image.[94] However, he bemoaned the fact that some women were not aware of their dignity because of their social and cultural conditioning.[95] He also called for the abolition of discrimination between girls and boys and called for an appreciation of the "genius of women."[96] For him, where women's dignity is not respected women have the responsibility to demand its recognition.[97] When the Holy Father addressed the African bishops in the year 2000, he

90. John Paul II, *World Day of Peace Message*, January 1995, §2. Pope John Paul II's documents not marked with a * have been sourced from the USCCB, *Pope John Paul II on the Genius of Women*, 5–113 (the numbers below reflect the paragraph numbers in the cited document).

91. Ibid., 7.

92. Ibid., 10.

93. John Paul II, *The Angelus Reflections: The Feminine Presence in the Family*, March 19, 1995, 2–3.

94. John Paul II, *The Angelus Reflections, Culture of Equality is Urgently Needed Today*, June 25, 1995, 1–3.

95. John Paul II, *World Day of Peace Message*. January 1995, 5.

96. John Paul II, *Letter to Women*, September. 1995, 8. *

97. John Paul II, *World Day of Peace Message*, January, 1995, 11.

emphasized the same message. He told them that men and women were different but equal in their humanity. In the same document, the Pope deplored some African customs and practices, which deprive women of their rights and the respect due to them.[98]

The Pope also encouraged equality between women and men that would result in equal pay for equal work and would render protection to working mothers since they are more vulnerable to workplace abuses. The equality had to be also seen in the rights of spouses through mutual respect not only as a matter of justice but also of necessity.[99] According to him, the dignity of women has a biblical and theological foundation in the incarnation of Jesus through Mary, an ordinary woman.[100] Pope John Paul II praised the vocation of women as mothers upon which the society is built. Women are the guardians of life.[101]

He also wrote the *Feminine Genius* in which he recognized the contribution of women in other spheres of human life. Women are to be allowed to develop to their full potential and the society should "strive convincingly to ensure that the widest possible space is open to women in all areas of culture, economics, politics, and ecclesial life itself so that human society is increasingly enriched by the gifts proper to masculinity and femininity.[102] He praised the complementarity and reciprocity between men and women.[103] The Pope condemned the exploitation and domination of women by men and encouraged humanity to learn from Jesus.[104] In his *Letter to Women* in September 1995, the Pope called for effective and intelligent campaigns for the promotion of women, an issue that he had explored and reiterated in his other documents.

This emphasis on the equality of men and women is very relevant to some African patriarchal societies in which women's dignity is not acknowledged and respected. When Pope John Paul II referred to women-unfriendly customs and traditions, he could have had in mind African customs and practices that either implicitly or explicitly demean women

98. John Paul II, *The Church in Africa: And Its Evangelizing Mission Towards the Year 2000* (Washington D.C: USCC, 2000), 82.

99. John Paul II, *Letter to Women*. September, 1995, 4.

100. John Paul II, *The Angelus Reflections: Culture of Equality is Urgently Needed Today*, June 25, 1995, 3.

101. John Paul II, *The Angelus Reflections: The Vocation to Motherhood*, July 16, 1995, 1–2.

102. Ibid., *The Feminine Genius*, July 23, 1995, 1.

103. John Paul II, *The Angelus Reflections: Complementarity's and Reciprocity between Women and Men*, July 9, 1995, para. 2.

104. John Paul II, *Letter to Women*, September 1995, 3.

and contribute to domestic violence. The message was a good sign from the Pope for women in Africa because he encouraged the bishops to do some soul searching to identify those cultural practices that were detrimental to the well-being of women.

Despite all that Pope John Paul II wrote about the equality between women and men, some scholars still find him wanting in the way he implemented what he wrote. Some critics accuse him of having failed to practice what he preached when it came to the leadership of women in the Roman Catholic Church. One of his most controversial messages concerning gender equality in church leadership is found in his final *Angelus Reflection* in which he revisited the thorny issue of women's role in the church. He made it clear that although women had a significant role to play in the church, the role of priesthood was closed to them.[105] From what the Pope had taught about women dignity in his other letters, many women had expected him to soften the church's position on the priesthood of women, but he did not.

The Pope's position on women's ordination led to his criticism for failing to do all within his authority to liberate women from being excluded from the most sacred office of the church. According to Melanie A. May, although women have participated actively in the daily life and sustenance of the church, they have too often served in subordinate positions. Leadership positions are reserved for men, and women only play secondary roles in the daily running of the church.[106] Women have worked tirelessly in the church and for the good of the people of God, but their position has not improved. Of course, many women have made great strides in the leadership and life of the church as religious sisters, but mostly as subordinates to their male counterparts. Some of them offer their unwavering service in the Vatican but in the periphery of mainstream church leadership.

Driven by the same anguish, Joanna Manning accuses the Vatican of treating women as objects of commentary and concern but not as serious people who can determine their own destiny. She bemoans the lack of evidence of Popes ever consulting women before writing their encyclicals.[107] For her, the Popes write what they feel about women without trying to listen to women's experiences and views first. While what she says may be true to some extent, it has been argued that at times it is difficult to consult women or their cultural representatives due to the many cultural differences and also because women at times do not speak with one voice. Despite that fact, women still think that there is no consultation, or that there is too little.

105. Ibid., 2.

106. May, ed., *Women and Church*, xviii.

107. Manning, *Is the Pope Catholic?*, 63.

Some women scholars have pointed out that the church's teaching about divorce is another way that the church has continued to disregard issues affecting women even during the Pontificate of John Paul II. The Roman Catholic Church's Catechism describes divorce as a "grave offense against the natural law" and condemns it as immoral.[108] This definition is offered without any qualification, and may encourage battered women to remain in abusive marriages because the church does not allow them to divorce. Although all Catholic marriages can be annulled, if there were certain impediments that prevented them from being valid marriage contracts at their very inception, but very few women and men know that.

Although some women scholars appreciate Pope John Paul II's favorable and positive writings about women, they point out that he was also on record for having closed the door to the discussion concerning women's ordination to the priesthood. Elizabeth A. Johnson has found the Roman Catholic Church magisterium wanting, especially Pope John Paul II when it comes to the ordination of women to the priesthood. Johnson criticizes the reasons given for disallowing women from becoming priests: "Why not? If women are genuinely human and if God is a deep mystery of holy love, then what is to prevent such an incarnation? But taking for granted the implicit inferiority of women, Christian theology has dignified maleness as the only genuine way of being human, thus making Jesus' embodiment as male an ontological necessity rather than a historical option."[109]

Despite all the criticism leveled against Pope John Paul II for his stance against the ordination of women to the priesthood that he inherited from his predecessors and tradition, some people still think that his work and campaigns for the dignity and equality of women has no parallel in the history of the Roman Catholic Church. Although he did not directly treat the topic of wife battering, he emphasized human dignity and equality in such a way that no one was left in doubt as to his stance against domestic violence. We can also infer that he would condemn it if he had addressed it directly just as he had condemned other types of violence, especially wars.

## The Zimbabwe Catholic Bishops' Conference on Women, Marriage, and Domestic Violence

The Zimbabwe Catholic Bishops' Conference has written several letters that make reference to marriage and violence, but only five letters will be considered in this section, namely: *Christian Marriage and Family Life*, 1984; *Male*

---

108. *Catechism of the Catholic Church*, 2384.

109. Johnson, *Consider Jesus*, 107.

*and Female He Created Them*, 1996; *God Hears the Cry of the Oppressed*, 2005; *The Zimbabwe We Want*, 2006; and *A Call to Conscience*, 2007. These pastoral letters are significant in this work because they deal with the equality of women and men, and the importance of marriage.

The Zimbabwe Catholic Bishop's Conference (ZCBC) in its letter, *Christian Marriage and Family Life*, 1984, start by reminding the Zimbabwe Catholics that the education of children in and by the family is an important part of the human and Christian development. The bishops state that it is the duty of both parents to educate children in the Christian way of life, particularly prayer. Both the father and mother of any Christian family have an equal responsibility to teach the children. The bishops encourage men to do their part effectively, instead of delegating all the teaching responsibilities to women.[110] For the bishops, one of the ways to teach children how to pray is by example. Children should be shown how to communicate with God not only by theory but by practicing it together as a family. Praying together can have the desirable result of bringing the family together. The bishops believe that prayer creates a strong relationship between family members and God, and that it has the power to draw the family together. For the bishops, praying as a family brings mutual respect among those who participate in it. In the same pastoral letter, the bishops call for marital fidelity, which is another crucial aspect of marital respect and dignity.[111] This fidelity automatically brings dignity to both the couple and marriage itself.

The bishops also encourage the sharing of ideas between the husband and wife. Sharing is an aspect of friendship. For the bishops, married couples should be best friends. Both the husband and wife have a lot of gifts that they bring to the union, and both partners should be willing to listen to the other to learn from the other and also to create a strong friendship through communication and dialogue as a way to cultivate a deeper and more meaningful love.[112] Every healthy marital relationship should involve giving and taking, listening and speaking, out of mutual respect and for mutual enrichment.

The pastoral letter also deals with leadership in the family in which men have traditionally been recognized as heads. The bishops agree with that, but instruct men to realize that their wives often have marked leadership ability in their own right and that husbands should be open to their wives' ideas and suggestions. According to the bishops, leadership qualities were not a monopoly of men alone. Neither men nor women possess a

---

110. ZCBC, *Christian Marriage and Family Life*, 1984.

111. Ibid.

112. Ibid.

monopoly of "intelligence, truth, or wisdom."[113] So, whoever, between the woman and the man, has a better idea, it should be respected. This mutual sharing of ideas calls for mutual respect between couples.

The bishops also write about the importance of children in a marriage and demonstrate their heartfelt sympathy for the barren women because of the strain that they have to endure in the Shona society. The bishops affirm that marriage without children suffers a strain because of natural and cultural expectations of marriage. They encourage childless couples to adopt children. The bishops show their support to the unmarried and divorced women. They also bemoan the terrible effects of divorce on children. They believe that divorce undermines the dignity of marriage. In the same letter, the bishops finally lamented the effects that expensive bridewealth has on Christian marriages. They asked for compassion from parents on those who wanted to marry. According to them, high-priced bridewealth was not in line with Christian principles.

The ZCBC in its letter, *Male and Female He Created Them*, 1996, reiterate the notion that Christian marriage is to be between men and women, and never to be between people of the same sex. They also revisit the equality and complementarity of men and women in marriage. For them, "Man was created for woman, and woman was created for man, and both were created for God. Man and woman are to complement each other. They are of equal dignity and value in the eyes of God, and yet different."[114] In the same letter, the bishops denounced homosexuality but upheld the right of homosexual people to live a life with freedom, without being harassed, persecuted, or tortured by anyone including the Zimbabwe government which at the time they were writing had shown a lot of animosity towards homosexuals.

Although the ZCBC wrote positively about marriage and women, in the above-mentioned documents, there are important issues, which they only dealt with in passing. Three of these were the issues of child adoption, divorce, and the payment of bridewealth. However, their emphasis on the dignity of married people and the equality of men and women was a significant development.

Neither has the ZCBC written directly against domestic violence, but this should not be interpreted to mean that the bishops of Zimbabwe have no concern for women and the issues of justice and women's liberation. They have written a great deal about human rights and problems of injustice, and they have also denounced political violence in Zimbabwe. By so doing, they

---

113. Ibid.

114. ZCBC, *Male and Female He Created Them*, 1996.

have implicitly criticized domestic violence in Zimbabwe because domestic violence has its roots in the denial of human rights to women by men.

In the bishops' 2006 joint document, which they produced with leaders of other Christian groups, they claim to have the responsibility to preach liberation to the marginalized. They also denounce domestic violence, though in passing. They reiterate that women and men are equal by having been created in the image of God.[115] They again denounce the domestication and subservience of women which they believe are not imposed by biological or any other natural necessity, not even by God, but are culturally constructed, and hence could be socially deconstructed.[116] This document gives evidence that the Christian leaders in Zimbabwe are aware of the sufferings that women undergo due to culturally constructed practices that are biased against them. They also accept the responsibility to liberate oppressed women, although they remind us that each Christian has a role to play.[117]

In their Lenten pastoral letter, *A Call to Metanoia: Listen to the Inner Voice*, 2003, the ZCBC calls for a change of heart, attitude, and mind. They call for a radical transformation of the structures of sin.[118] This call is a good sign and shows that the bishops have the authority to challenge social and economic structures, which marginalize and oppress women.

## Comments

This chapter has highlighted some attitudes and teachings about women from the Catholic traditional perspective. It has been established that the Roman Catholic Church has both supported women and denigrated them in its traditions. Some scholars believe that the contradictory teaching of the church on women has had both negative and positive results on the position of women in society. Some people have utilized the negative teachings and practices to the disadvantage of women. Others have used the positive teachings to liberate women from male dominance and marginalization. Although it has been noted that the religious tradition has ostracized women and kept them on the periphery of church leadership, it has sufficient resources that can be used to liberate women. The New Testament writings, as the foundational writings of the church, have adequate theological support for the dignity of women and their equality with men.

---

115. ZCBC, EFZ, and ZCC, *The Zimbabwe We Want*, 2–3.

116. Ibid., 3.2.10.

117. McBrien, "An Ecclesiology for Women and Men," 29.

118. ZCBC, *A Call to Metanoia*, 4.

Although much has not been said about domestic violence in the religious tradition that has been explored, the emancipation of women that the religious tradition espouses denounces all negative attitudes towards women. Anything that may lead to the demeaning of women and the undermining of their dignity, such as domestic violence is against the principles of the gospel. In our society, there is nothing that undermines the dignity of women more than domestic violence does, and because of that, all the practices that promote it should be challenged, transformed or even abolished. However, it should be noted that liberation of any kind is a long process because oppressors do not give away their privileges without a fight.

# Chapter 5

## The Theological Conversation

CHAPTERS 1, 2, AND 3 of this book explored the experiences of the Shona women in Zimbabwe regarding domestic violence and the cultural practice of bridewealth that happen within the marriage set up. Chapter 4 dealt with the religious tradition, particularly the teachings and writings on women by Jesus Christ, Paul, church fathers, popes, and some bishops of the Roman Catholic Church. Chapter 4's objective was to find out if we can tap into that religious tradition in our endeavor to liberate the Shona women. Although the Christian tradition that has been explored has not always spoken with one voice concerning the dignity of women, there is still a lot of good lessons that can be gleaned from it to emancipate Shona women from some cultural practices that might undermine their dignity.

Chapter 5 deals with the second phase of the theological reflection that was propounded and expounded by James D. Whitehead and Evelyn Eaton Whitehead that has a model and a method. The model "instigates a conversation among three sources of religiously relevant information—the experience of the community of faith, the Christian tradition, and the resources of the culture."[1] The religious tradition as a source of theological reflection includes, but is not limited to the pronunciations of the church, church councils, Christian history, denominational history, theological, and doctrinal statements.[2] This theological reflection requires all the three dialoguing voices, namely, personal or communal experience, culture, and religious tradition to have a conversation about the subject in question.[3]

1. Whitehead and Whitehead, *Method in Ministry*, 6.
2. Ibid.
3. Ibid., 13–14.

The employment of the religious tradition in doing theological reflection shows the need for theological continuity in Christian communities. Although the Christian community's experiences and context might be different from its religious tradition, it may find wisdom in finding out how similar experiences were dealt with by its tradition in the past. So, whenever a current community experiences something that needs the community's attention, it is sometimes beneficial to go back to its religious traditions for inspiration and wisdom.

The second voice or partner in this theological conversation is the experience of both the individual and community that prompts some theological discernment and response from the community. According to the Whiteheads, "pastoral reflection begins as we confront an urgent concern, a pressing issue arising in personal or communal experience."[4] To some extent, theological reflection is ignited by some personal or communal experience that compels believers to ask questions such as, "where is God in all this? What does the church say about this experience?" What does the Bible say about what's happening to me or us? Can we learn anything from our cultural heritage that can help us deal with the situation that we are facing?" The moment an individual or community begins to seek answers to such questions that is the beginning of a theological reflection.

The third partner in the theological dialogue is culture. Although scholars do not agree on the definition of culture, they concur that it includes things such as values, religion, ethics, philosophy, cosmology, food, songs, art, economics, politics, and many others. Every individual or community that is experiencing an issue that calls for theological reflection has its own culture. The Shona people had a culture that kept them going for thousands of years before the arrival of Christianity. Consequently, when they are trying to find a solution to a problem that bedevils their community, they need also to tap into their cultural resources. They should scrutinize their culture to find out if there is any cultural practice that exacerbates the problem under discussion so that it can be challenged or transformed. The positive aspects of culture should be embraced and the negative purified.

How do we apply the above model to the issue that is under discussion? We start with the experiences of domestic violence, marriage, and bridewealth among the Shona. As people continue to encounter domestic violence, they begin to ask questions such as, "what is marriage? Are Shona men and women equal? What does emancipation mean for the Shona? What does the Bible teach about violence, marriage, equality, and bridewealth? What does the Shona culture say about marriage, equality, emancipation,

---

4. Ibid., 7.

and bridewealth? Is the payment of bridewealth in line with the principles of the gospel of Jesus Christ of love, human dignity, freedom, and peace?" These questions ignite a theological conversation or reflection that may lead to a pastoral response.

In addition to the model, the Whiteheads propose a threefold method to the above theological reflection process, which has three parts, namely, *attending, assertion,* and *pastoral response. Attending* refers to the uninterrupted and non-judgmental listening to the experiences and insights of those who are affected by the issue that is under reflection.[5] In this case, the issue concerns domestic violence and one of its contributing factors—bridewealth. These experiences can be found in books, survivors' stories, newspapers, and other media. They are experiences of individuals or communities. They are the experiences of the dehumanization, exploitation, subjugation, abuse, and oppression of Shona women. *Attending* has already been dealt with in chapters, 1, 2, and 3. Chapter 3 also explored the cultural practice of bridewealth to find out the extent to which it contributes to domestic violence. *Assertion* stipulates that the voices in the conversation be brought into a dialogue that may have both agreements and differences.[6] The aim of this dialogue is to give each voice an opportunity to either affirm or criticize what other voices have to say about domestic violence, marriage, and bridewealth for the purpose of coming up with viable pastoral strategies. Hence, the final part of the method is the pastoral response, which seeks to bring about a practical resolution to the challenges that are being experienced by the individual or the community.[7] Every fruitful theological reflection should lead the engaged people from mere insight and discussion to the implementation of the plans that they formulate. James D. and Evelyn E. Whitehead have warned that sometimes such a conversation may not bear any tangible fruits, and because of that, those who are engaged in such a theological reflection should go back to the drawing board and start all over.

For the sake of clarity, this correlation will be centered on the following questions: What is marriage? Are Shona women and men equal? What does it mean to be emancipated? The dialoguing partners will respond to the questions in the following order: experience, culture, and religious tradition. In this exercise, experience refers to individual and communal theoretical views by scholars about marriage, equality, and emancipation. Culture refers to the Shona cultural practices, particularly marriage and bridewealth,

---

5. Whitehead and Whitehead, *Method in Ministry*, 13.

6. Ibid., 14–16.

7. Ibid., 16.

and religious tradition deals with the views of the Roman Catholic Church concerning marriage, gender equality, humanity dignity, and emancipation of women. At the end of each part of the dialogue, a summary of similarities and differences will be drawn. It is hoped that the similarities and differences will lead to the formulation of a relevant pastoral response. It should be noted that most of the material that will be revisited in this chapter has already been discussed in other chapters.

## What is a Marriage?

### Experience

A Shona marriage can be defined as an institution in which women and men enter a conjugal union for the purpose of procreating and companionship. Bridewealth has to be paid to the relatives of the woman so that the marriage can be validated. Marriage has to be consummated by the bearing of children, at least, one of whom is a boy. For the Shona, marriage is an obligation for everyone who is physically able because it is believed to be an institution that gives immortality to both the individual and the lineage. The Shona marriage starts with the first payment of bridewealth, a ritual that starts before the woman begins to live with the man, and is completed many years into the marriage. Although the Shona marriage is revocable, the assumption is that both parties will do all in their power to keep the marriage going even where there are challenges.

### Culture

Adrian Hastings has defined the African marriage as "union, permanent at least by intention, of a man and a woman for the purpose of the procreation and rearing of children and mutual companionship and assistance."[8] The Shona culture acknowledges that marriage is an important institution that was established by their ancestors for everyone, without exception. Under normal circumstances every one of marriageable age should marry because marriage is a duty to the community as a whole through which the family, lineage, and clan are assured of continuity. John S. Mbiti has stated it concisely as follows: "Therefore, marriage is a duty, a requirement from the corporate society, and a rhythm of life in which everyone must participate. Otherwise, he who does not participate in it is a curse to the community, he is a rebel and a law-breaker, he is not only abnormal but, "under-human."

8. Hastings, *Christian Marriage in Africa*, 27.

Failure to get married under normal circumstances means that the person concerned has rejected society and society rejects him in turn."[9]

The Shona derogatorily refer to a man who willingly abstains from marriage and has passed the expected marriageable age as *tsvimborume*.[10] John S. Mbiti thinks that since marriage and procreation are the gateways to immortality among African people, those who forego it are choosing death instead of life. The marriage has to be only between women and men. Those men and women of homosexual orientation are expected to marry, heterosexually so that they can bear children. The Shona marriage contract is a long process in which two groups, wife-givers and wife-receivers, together with the concerned individuals exchange their consent.[11] The whole extended family is involved in one way or the other. The duty to find suitable marriage partners is left to the individuals who intend to marry in most instances, but their whole families are involved in the exchange of the marriage consent.[12]

The payment of bridewealth plays an important role in marriage negotiations without which marriage would be invalid. The bridewealth is paid in parts, and its payment gives the man full rights over the wife and her children. There is a consensus among the Shona that bridewealth has gone through a lot of changes and in the process, it has become commercialized, distorted, corrupted, and too expensive. This transition has influenced some Shona men to act as if they would have *purchased* their wives. As a result of that mentality, some men may treat their wives in any manner that they deem fit.

The Shona culture emphasizes the importance of children in any marriage union. Failure to beget children is a cause for concern. Barrenness poses a significant challenge to a marriage union. Barrenness, among the Shona, is a cause for the dissolution of marriage unless the wife's relatives are willing to give the son-in-law another wife to bear children for him on behalf of her barren sister. This arrangement was intended to save the wife-givers from refunding some of the bridewealth that they would have received. This does not mean that every childless marriage fails because many such marriages have survived the test of time, but not without challenges.

---

9. Mbiti, African *Religions and Philosophy*, 174.

10. *Tsvimborume* is a compound word that comes from two Shona words, *tsvimbo* (walking stick), and *murume* (man). Literarily, *tsvimborume* refers to a man who is always holding his walking stick. Symbolically, it refers to a man who by necessity gets his sexual gratification from masturbation.

11. Bourdillon, *The Shona Peoples*, 37.

12. Ibid., 36.

Although the traditional Shona considered marriage to be permanent, they entered it with the full knowledge that it could be dissolved if certain conditions were not met. Adrian Hastings remarks that "Among nearly all peoples of Africa marriage was in general intention lifelong but was also in principle dissoluble . . ."[13] The husband, wife, and their families could agree to the dissolution of a marriage because of one or more of the following reasons: the son-in-law's failure to pay bridewealth, death of the wife or the husband, barrenness of the wife, impotency of the husband, infidelity of the wife or husband, accusation of witchcraft against the wife, and others. In the case of a divorce, the husband or wife had to give the partner who is being divorced a token of divorce, known as *gupuro*, to show that he or she wanted the marriage to be dissolved.[14] This token of divorce was in the form of a small amount of money, for instance, one dollar. The marriage dissolution discussions would follow and usually the intention of such discussions was to save and restore the union, but if the husband or the wife or the parents of either wife or husband insisted that the marriage was to be dissolved, then it had to be granted. So, among the Shona, marriage is a dissoluble contract between the wife-givers and wife-receivers that is validated by the payment of bridewealth and is consummated through the birth of an adequate number of children.

## Roman Catholic Church Religious Tradition

Marriage has been defined as a union between a woman and a man that was established by God for the purpose of procreation and companionship. In his letter, *Mulieris Dignitatem* (August 15, 1988), Pope John Paul II wrote that God had instituted marriage "as an indispensable condition for the transmission of life to new generations, the transmission of life to which marriage and conjugal love are by their nature ordered . . ."[15]

The Roman Catholic Church (RCC) categorically teaches that children are the primary purpose of marriage although a marriage is expected to remain intact even in their absence.[16] *The Pastoral Constitution on the Church in the Modern World, Gaudium et Spes*, Vatican II, has put it clearly that the purpose of marriage is to procreate and educate the children. It recognizes that children are the gift of marriage and greatly contribute to the welfare of

13. Hastings, *Christian Marriage in Africa*, 35.

14. Holleman, *Shona Customary Law*, 265–323. *Gupuro* could be in the form of money or an article such as a hoe.

15. John Paul II, *Mulieris Dignitatem*, 6.

16. Shorter, *African Culture and the Christian Church*, 182.

the parents. Procreation and the education of children are married couples' divine mission. Be that as it may, the constitution stipulates that marriage remains indissoluble even in situations where there are no children.[17] Likewise, the ZCBC acknowledges that without children marriage suffers strain, but it remains a life-long undertaking, and the bishops encourage childless couples to adopt children instead of resorting to polygyny or divorce.[18]

The above teaching demonstrates that children are very important to a marriage union, and the lack of children may result in adverse consequences to a marriage. Religious tradition has always emphasized the importance of families as *domestic churches* in which children receive their first education.[19] The RCC acknowledges the goodness of the family and has taught that both the husband and the wife are partners in the education of their children. The ZCBC has taught that the future of the church and humanity depend on the type and caliber of the families.[20] To emphasize this point, the bishops quoted Pope John Paul II's speech in Accra Ghana: "Let every family be a domestic Church, a community where the Lord Jesus has a central place, where children learn to know and love God, where prayer is the binding force. In this community of love and life, the future of society is decided and the peace of the world is built."[21]

The Catholic Church religious tradition teaches that marriage between two individuals begins with the willing exchange of consents by those intending to marry before an official witness of the church and two other witnesses.[22] The matrimonial consent has been defined as "an act of the will by which a man and a woman mutually give and accept each other in an irrevocable covenant for the purpose of establishing marriage."[23] If matrimonial "consent is lacking or defective, whether on the part of one or both parties, the marriage is invalid" and it can be annulled.[24]

The marriage contract takes place within a short period, and immediately after the exchange of marriage vows the man and woman are pronounced husband and wife and from that point they can proceed to consummate their union.[25] This union remains dissoluble until it is con-

---

17. Vatican Council II, *Gaudium et Spes*, no. 50.

18. ZCBC, *Christian Marriage and Family Life*, 1984, no. 2.

19. *Catechism of the Catholic Church*, 1656–58.

20. ZCBC, *Christian marriage and Family Life*, 1984, no. 3.

21. Ibid.

22. Caparros et al., eds., *Code of Canon Law Annotated*, can. 1057.

23. Huels, *The Pastoral Companion*, 233; can. 1057.

24. Ibid.

25. Shorter, *African Culture and the Christian Church*, 182.

summated by the sexual intercourse between the married couple. Once it is consummated, the marriage cannot be dissolved except if either party or both can prove, beyond any reasonable doubt that there were particular impediments that existed at the time of the contracting of the marriage, which render the marriage null and void.[26]

According to the Roman Catholic Church, marriage between two baptized persons is a sacrament.[27] Marriage should be free from impediments or lack of form, and must be entered by two consenting adults if it is to be valid. "A marriage can be invalid for any of the three general reasons: the presence of an impediment, lack of required form, or defective consent."[28]

The RCC religious tradition teaches that perpetuity is an essential characteristic of marriage by the law of nature.[29] According to Gerard Taylor, Canon law stipulates that marriages that can be dissolved by the Pope are those that are not ratified and not consummated, if one of the parties is baptized at the time of the dissolution (Petrine Privilege).[30] A marriage can also be dissolved through the Pauline privilege if it is between two unbaptized persons, "in favor of the faith of the party who received baptism by the very fact that a new marriage is contracted by that party, provided the unbaptized departs."[31]

## Similarities and Differences

All the three voices namely, experience, culture, and RCC tradition agree that marriage is a union between a woman and a man and that marriage is paramount for the continuation of the human race and companionship. All agree that it was ordained by the Supreme Being who for the RCC is God, and for Shona traditionalists, could be the same God or the Great Ancestor. They agree that children that may become the fruit of marriage union are very significant and that barrenness or sterility may bring strain to marriage. For marriage to be ratified, some form of contract should be entered into with a willing exchange of consents by those concerned.

Despite the above commonalities, there are some disagreements among the dialoguing partners. The Shona culture traces marriage back to

26. *Code of Canon Law Annotated*, can. 1061.

27. Huels, *The Pastoral Companion*, 189; can. 1059.

28. Ibid., 235; can. 1073.

29. Ibid., 245; can. 1056.

30. Taylor, "Recent Developments in Canonical Legislation, Jurisprudence and Church Practice: Declaration of Nullity and Dissolution Cases," 74.

31. Huels, *The Pastoral Companion*, 276; Can. 1143.

the ancestors, and this makes marriage a human product. The RCC traces marriage to God, who might be the same or different from the Great Ancestor. However, some African Traditional Religion scholars have tried to harmonize the Christian God and the Great Ancestor by arguing that they are one and the same being.

Another difference concerns the concept of marital consent. The voice of experience agrees that there should be the exchange of consent between those individuals who intend to live together as husband and wife. Culture is divided, with some people saying that the marital consent should be given by the marriage couple, and others arguing that the exchange of marital consent should receive family approval. Since bridewealth validates a Shona marriage, if the relatives of the woman refuse to accept it, then there is nothing the man and the woman can do.

According to the RCC, the exchange of marital consents is the culmination of the free choices made by the couple in choosing a marriage partner. But, for the Shona, the consent is between those individuals intending to marry with the express approval of their families. Moreover, although the marriage partners' freedom to choose a partner is respected, the choice may be vetoed by their families. If the parents refuse to give their consent to a marriage union then, the marriage might not go forward. For the RCC, the marital consents should be given by those individuals who intend to marry, and it is the two persons' absolute right to do so. Once the two individuals say to each other "I do, I do" and there is no canonical defect in their consents, the required form is followed, and neither of them is rendered by a "diriment impediment incapable of contracting a marriage validly," then, the contract is sealed.[32]

The consummation of a Shona marriage is a long process that may take many years. The married couple is not allowed to enjoy certain of the marital rights and other privileges until the bridewealth is paid. A couple may wed in the church, but the marriage would not be consummated customarily until satisfactory bridewealth is paid, and the adequate number of children are born. The RCC marriage contract is different from that of Shona culture in the sense that it takes place and is finalized during a short period. The married couple acquires marital rights immediately after the exchange of vows.

Another difference concerns the payment of bridewealth. The RCC tradition does not recognize the payment of bridewealth as a significant aspect of a sacramental marriage. However, the RCC pastors are aware of the fact that some Shona parents demand the payment of bridewealth

---

32. Huels, *The Pastoral Companion,* 209; can. 1073.

before the bride's parents can allow a church wedding to take place. Because of that the issue of bridewealth has remained a thorn in the flesh to those who intend to wed in the RCC. Roman Catholics know that what makes a marriage irrevocable is the church wedding, not the payment of bridewealth and because of that they then try to make sure that the church wedding does not take place until bridewealth is paid.[33] The typical procedure is for the customary marriage negotiations to precede the church wedding. Some Shona couples who do not have the permission to wed in the church from the wife's relatives may secretly do it without the consent of the bride's parents provided the priest is willing to officiate.

The RCC teaches that sterility of either party or both does not invalidate matrimonial consent unless if the sterility was fraudulently concealed to obtain the consent of the other party.[34] If sterility is discovered later in marriage, the RCC tradition suggests that either the couple remains childless or adopts a child. The Shona culture does not condone the adoption of children although a couple may take care of their relatives' children, but never with the intention of making the children legally their own.

The dissolution of a marriage brings another difference to the conversation. Experience agrees that marriage may be dissolved because of barrenness, infidelity, or for other reasons. Culturally, a marriage may not be dissolved because of infidelity, but it may be dissolved because of barrenness or failure by the son-in-law to pay all of the bridewealth. Ratification and consummation of the Shona traditional marriage require many years. The RCC tradition teaches that a sacramental marriage that is both ratified and consummated cannot be dissolved. This is a dilemma for those people who follow both the Shona culture and the RCC tradition because the Shona culture allows them to dissolve their marriages, yet, the RCC tradition does not.

There is agreement too. First, the voice of experience and the Shona culture agree that bridewealth should be paid and failure to do so makes the union illicit. Most women, if not all, want bridewealth to be paid for them. Many think that bridewealth adds value to them and raise their status in their families and the Shona society. They know that unless bridewealth is paid for them, their relatives will never recognize their marriages as legitimate. Some relatives of the woman confirm this myth by rendering more respect to the daughter who would have fetched more bridewealth than the one who would have fetched none.

33. Mair, *Marriage*, 95.
34. Huels, *The Pastoral Companion,* 220; can. 1059.

Second, all three voices agree that children are crucial in marriage. However, they differ as to what should be done in the event of a childless union. The voice of experience argues that divorce or an extramarital affair is the answer. The Shona culture insists on having children at all costs or otherwise the marriage should be dissolved. Marriage is consummated by the actual births of several children, and not merely by the sexual act. In the past, in the case of an infertile husband, his young brother would be asked to have clandestine sex with his brother's wife to bear children for him. However, both experience and religious tradition condemn this as adultery. Culturally, in the case of a barren wife, another woman, usually, the wife's young sister would be offered to the husband to bear children for her barren sister. This phenomenon automatically leads to polygyny that both experience and the RCC tradition condemn as criminal and sinful, respectively.[35]

## Are Shona Women and Men Equal?

### *Experience*

Many people are of the opinion that the equality between women and men is a necessity that is demanded by the modern way of life. Although Shona women acknowledge the existence of differences between women and men, they desire the equality and mutual respect between the husband and the wife. Mutual respect demands that both spouses do not act in a way that encourages the subordination of the other partner. Mutual respect would require that the husband does not do something to the wife that he does not want his wife to do to him. Domestic violence occurs when the couple does not observe the Golden Rule of reciprocity. Failure to acknowledge the equality between the man and the woman may encourage domestic violence.

Some people are concerned about the equality of women and men at workplaces and in public offices. It has been argued that women and men should be allowed to take up employment if they are qualified and that they should receive equal salaries for the same work. In Zimbabwe, there are jobs and professions that are seen as either feminine or masculine. However, some people feel that no profession should be exclusive to a particular gender. Even at home both men and women should do domestic chores and take care of the children together. There should not be household chores that Shona men should not do. There are situations where both the wife and husband are employed, and when the two come home from work the man

---

35. Kisembo et al., *African Christian Marriage*, 104–7.

sits down and reads his newspaper while the wife is expected to cook for the family, do laundry, and bath the children.

Many feel that women should be given an opportunity to occupy top positions in public offices if gender equality is to be recognized. Top positions would allow women to make decisions and policies that would benefit ordinary women. For instance, until recently, Zimbabwe professional training institutions such as Teachers' Training Colleges and Nursing Training Schools, had the practice of suspending women for becoming pregnant during the course of the program, even if they were married, but they would not do the same to the man responsible for the pregnancy even if he were a student at the same institution. Such policies are challenged by women when they are given the necessary voice and authority. Women should be encouraged to acquire the necessary academic qualifications and professional training, and to occupy managerial and administrative positions at work places and in political leadership.

Some people agree that although gender equality is vital, it should be acknowledged that men remain the heads of the families. Some scholars argue that men's traditional task of protecting the woman and children should continue.[36] This role is more important in a country like Zimbabwe where the unemployment rate is more than 80%, and where the majority of women are not gainfully employed. However, men's headship does not mean that men should do things alone but rather in consultation with their wives. If necessity demands it, women should also become the heads of the households with the help of their husbands. There seems to be a conflict between emphasizing men's headship and the need for gender equality.

The equality of property ownership should be encouraged, and the responsibility for the children should belong to both parents and in the event of a divorce, the courts should decide who would have the custody of the children. Men should not be allowed to have a monopoly of ultimate responsibility for the children, which seems to be the current practice of the Shona customary law. Some women also feel that equality between women and men should extend to conjugal rights. Most women argue that both men and women should be entitled to the sexual exclusivity of their spouse and that women should be allowed to negotiate matters of reproduction with men. Some of those who support gender balance believe that this equality comes from God, who created men and women equally in his image.

36. Fox, *Kinship and Marriage*, 37–39.

## Culture

In the Shona culture, the question of the equality between women and men was not usually discussed directly. Consequently, the Shona culture's response to the question of gender equality could only be inferred from their views on kinship, women, marriage, and family. The Shona society is patriarchal and because of that, some men consider themselves to be above the females. Children born in all Shona marriages take the totem of the father and are believed to belong to him.

The other issue at stake is the concept of the family. According to Shorter, there are two types of families, namely, nuclear in which the family unit is reduced to the husband, wife and children; and the other is the extended family in which the family includes a relatively large group of those related by descent and marriage.[37] The Shona follow the extended family type whose smallest unit is the nuclear family. The husband is believed to be the head of the household because he pays bridewealth for the woman. The Shona know that the payment of bridewealth gives men absolute rights over women and children, and it places the wife in a permanent submissive position. The husband may marry many wives but the wife cannot do the same. Furthermore, there is a clear division of labor. Women work in the fields, cook for the family, and look after the children. Equality means that both men and women should remain faithful to their calling and respective duties.

## Roman Catholic Church Religious Tradition

In recent times, the RCC tradition has been unwavering in its insistence that both women and men were created in the image of God and because of that, they are equal. Pope John Paul II wrote that the fact that human beings were created as man and woman in the image of God means that each of them individually is like God and they should live in unity and love.[38] Equality requires that women have to be treated with dignity that proceeds from being created in the image of God. Jesus treated women who followed him with dignity, respect, and as equals of the men who followed him. Paul, who came after Jesus, also treated women and men in much the same way. He respected women and allowed some of them to be his coworkers. Tertullian, who is a Church Father, treated women as equals and had respect for women. Pope John Paul II wrote many letters insisting on the equality of women and

---

37. Shorter, *African Culture and the Christian Church*, 163–64.
38. *Mulieris Dignitatem*, 7.

men. In his welcome message to Gertrude Mongella, Secretary-General of the Fourth World Conference on Women, to the Vatican on May 26, 1995, he pointed out that equality of dignity does not mean sameness because that would impoverish women and all of society by undermining the crucial and irreplaceable role that women play.[39] In the same message, Pope John Paul II reiterated what he wrote elsewhere that "profound changes are needed in the attitudes and organization of society in order to facilitate the participation of women in public life, while at the same time providing for the special obligations of women and men with regard to their families."[40]

Religious tradition demands the elimination of discrimination against women in areas that include education, health care, and employment.[41] The RCC tradition has emphasized the dignity of women that should be recognized not only by women but also by men. It says that any man who offends a woman's dignity, in fact, undermines his own dignity.[42] Pope John Paul II lamented the fact that history is filled with men's achievements and victories, but there is little or nothing said about the contributions and sacrifices of women.[43] Although the RCC is still convinced that the husband is the leader of the household, it acknowledges the importance of the woman's input, and that the husband should be open to his wife's ideas and suggestions because leadership qualities, intelligence, truth, and wisdom are not a monopoly of men.[44]

One of the challenges that some Shona households face is that, even if the woman displays more leadership qualities than the husband, she still may be discouraged from being the leader of the family. She may suggest meaningful ideas but the husband as the traditionally recognized head of the family may reject them. This scenario seems to undermine the equality between men and women that the church preaches about. Probably the question of leadership or headship of the family needs to be revisited and redefined so that this can also be merited rather than being inherited because of one's gender. Family leadership could be shared more equally between the husband and wife if men understand that either the wife or the husband can lead the household if she or he has the intelligence and wisdom to do it. It should be noted that many Shona families are experimenting with

39. John Paul II, *Welcome to Gertrude Mongella, Secretary General of the Fourth World Conference on Women*, May 26, 1995, 3.

40. Ibid., 5.

41. Ibid., 6.

42. *Mulieris Dignitatem*, 10.

43. Ibid.

44. Ibid., 5.

collaborative leadership in which the man and woman consult each other in making decisions for the family, and many have found this model much rewarding.

## Similarities and Differences

To some extent, the voices of experience and the RCC agree that women and men are equal. That equality is derived from the Judeo-Christian creation story where God created both the woman and the man in his own image. All the three voices also agree that the man is the head of the family, and that women should be treated with dignity. The three voices agree that collaborative leadership in which the husband and the wife consult each other before making significant decisions for the family, is the most rewarding model of running the family.

However, there are more differences than similarities. The RCC tradition categorically teaches that men and women are equal, but the equality that the RCC tradition supports exclude the equality in ministry. According to the RCC tradition women cannot be ordained to the priesthood, and because of that, some women have accused the RCC tradition of inconsistency. Yes, they want women to occupy leadership position in the society but not in the church. For the church, women can occupy leadership positions in any area in the society, but not in the church because Jesus Christ did not choose any woman to be an apostle. Yes, women can lead parish councils and other institutions of the church, but without being ordained to the priesthood, they may never become bishops, cardinals, or popes.

If the equality between men and women is to be taken seriously then, the rights gained by the spouses in marriage should be mutual. According to Jean Stapleton and Richard Bright, equality in marriage "means having the same status in the relationship, the same responsibility for success of the relationship, and the same responsibility for the couple's survival in the world."[45] It is not like that in the Shona culture. The Shona culture permits men to have sexual exclusivity over their wives, but not the other way round. But, the RCC tradition demands reciprocal sexual exclusivity. In *Humanae Vitae*, Pope Paul VI taught that "married life is faithful and exclusive of all other and this until death."[46] Here, both the man and the woman are seen as equal partners when it comes to these rights.

---

45. Stapleton and Bright, *Equal Marriage*, 13.

46. Paul VI, *The Encyclical Letter of the Regulation of Births, Humane Vitae*, 25 July 1968, 9.

The RCC also teaches that the children, who are the fruits of marriage belong to both the mother and the father and that both parents have the responsibility to educate them about faith. In the event of the marriage breaking up, the courts of the land may decide who the custodian of the children should be after considering the best interests of the children. Although the battle for the custody of the children is bitter in every culture, but once the law of the land has decided on the custody of the child, all the parties involved must comply. If either of the involved spouses violates the ruling of the courts, the courts have the means of enforcing their ruling. It's different among the Shona, some of whom find it difficult to accept the ruling of the courts concerning the custody of the children after divorce because they have another way of looking at the marriage contract. At the core of the customary marriage law is the payment of bridewealth that gives the man absolute rights over the ownership of the children. The wife may win the custody of the children in a court of law, but she is always reminded that the children belong to their father and that they must go back to their father.

Although all three voices agree that the man is the head of the family, nevertheless all differ in the way they define this headship. For Shona culture, that male primacy gives the man arbitrary powers, even to the point of disciplining the wife by beating. Hence, women and men become unequal. For the RCC tradition, the headship of the husband is not clear, but it seems that the church expects the spouses to employ collaborative leadership that calls for the consultation between the man and the woman. The ZCBC has clearly encouraged married men to accept and respect their wives' wisdom and ideas.

The voice of experience is divided. Some people side with Shona culture and others with the RCC religious tradition. This diversity shows that the contemporary Shona people are divided between the callings of their traditional past and the teachings of the Christian tradition. A non-collaborative and non-consultative household headship by the men leaves no room for equality between the spouses in marriage. Because of that, some Shona men believe that if the woman does not want to accept the husband's headship she should be coerced to do so using whatever means necessary. The myth of coercive headship is widespread among some Shona young men, who believe that the leadership of the husband should be established through the instilling of fear in the wife. This mentality shows that some Shona men do not respect equality in marriage.

There is also a difference in the way that the dignity of the woman should be recognized and upheld. The RCC tradition teaches that this dignity is realized when the woman's rights as a human being created in the image of God are respected and upheld. The voice of experience has it that the woman's dignity should be marked by the end of domestic violence in any form, and when women can define their own destiny. For culture, the woman obtains her dignity in accord with the dictates of the husband and his relatives and by remaining in her place as a woman. Her dignity is in the bearing and taking care of children, being faithful to her husband, and carrying out her other marital responsibilities unwaveringly. It seems that in marriage, the woman should earn her dignity, but the man inherits it from patriarchy.

## What Does Women's Emancipation Mean?

### Experience

The *Webster's New Universal Unabridged Dictionary* defines emancipation as "the act of setting free from slavery, servitude, or restraint; deliverance from bondage or controlling influence; liberation. . ."[47] Mercy Amba Oduyoye has defined woman emancipation, as women's refusal to stay on the margins by reclaiming their humanity. For her, emancipation deals with the transformation of the patriarchal society and the church.[48] For most ordinary Shona women, emancipation means self-determination and freedom from male domination, exploitation, and subjugation. It means equality between spouses. This patriarchal domination of women by men leads some men to treat women as if they were sub-humans. It allows men in all spheres of life to make major decisions about women and the children without much consideration for women's needs and opinions. Emancipation means deliverance from bad male controlling influences that stifle human development. It means freedom from gender discrimination and restriction. Some Shona men restrict their wives to homes even if the women do not enjoy it. Men can limit the friends that women can have, and the money women can spend. Emancipation means respect of women's talents, dignity, aspirations, decision making capacity, and wisdom. For some women, emancipation means the reversal of duties between men and women. Some people have criticized this perspective for attempting to overthrow the natural order of creation. However, many women advocate the complementarity of men and women whereby they can assist each other in running their families with mutual respect. Women's emancipation calls for the restoration of women's dignity that domestic violence has ruined so grievously.

---

47. McKechnie, ed., *Webster's New Universal Unabridged Dictionary*, 590.
48. Oduyoye, *Introducing African Women's Theology*, 76, 116.

Women do not agree on the ways that should be used to restore their lost dignity. Some call for the incarceration of perpetrators of domestic violence. Some women have noted with concern the consequences of the confinement of an abusive husband who is the breadwinner of the family. Other women think that emancipation will be brought about by allowing divorce in circumstances where the wife is abused. Some activists encourage women to fight back their abusive husbands. Some women have called for affirmative action that seeks to empower women by giving them priority in opportunities that concern education, employment, and other economic, political, and social spheres that are dominated by men. Some have suggested the re-education of men about human dignity and gender equality by challenging some cultural practices that undermine the dignity of women. There are also women who encourage other women to accept the patriarchal status quo as God-given, and to be countenanced without complaining. They do not want anybody to rock the patriarchal boat, but to take a fatalistic stance by accepting the position of women as their destiny.

## *Culture*

Even though the emancipation of women was not openly and explicitly discussed in Shona culture, there was always a desire to have families live in harmony. Young boys were instructed to respect their sisters. Newly wedded men knew that their wives were to be treated with dignity. For them, emancipation meant the freedom of the women to perform their part in running the family without unhealthy interference from the husband. Although there were men who interfered with women's domestic work such as cooking, everybody was aware that choosing what to cook for the family was the woman's jurisdiction.

It is true that some forms of domestic violence were allowed, but when they exceeded the levels that were considered to be moderate, other people intervened to liberate the woman. In some cases, the relatives of the abused woman were willing to pay back some of the cattle and money that they would have received as bridewealth from their son-in-law to pave way for a divorce. The relatives of the man also tried to restore peace and order to their son's family by educating him on how to live amicably with his wife. Whenever they thought that the man was treating his wife unfairly, they would challenge him, and at times, demanded that he stopped it.

Emancipation also meant forgiveness. The Shona community was willing to forgive those women who were found wanting in one way or the other provided they promised to repent. The society was aware that women were human beings, and at times transgressed the moral standards of the society. The realization that women were human enough to sin was in itself liberating. For instance, a woman who was caught in adultery was sometimes forgiven provided she confessed her offence, named her secret lover, and was willing to transform her ways. A woman who was barren was not divorced at once, but there were mechanisms that were put in place to make sure that the situation was dealt with without making the woman a social outcast. Those women who could not perform some of their marital duties such as cooking were given an opportunity to go back to their relatives, particularly aunts, to learn how to execute their duties efficiently. So, just knowing that there were so many people who wished to see the marriage prosper was liberating to the woman.

It should be noted that in the past, the emancipation of women did not mean giving unchecked freedom to women to work in the newly introduced mines, industries, and commercial farms. Most women had to stay in the home taking care of the children. The home protected the woman from the harsh and treacherous environment of the job industry. Staying at home liberated them from some of the indignities working women face on the job market such as unequal salaries and sexual assaults. Women had to be respected for the significant part that they played in the home. Emancipation was not tantamount to the freedom to wear miniskirts, but to dress in a manner that showed the sacredness and honor of the Shona women. Yes, in the home some women still faced exploitation, but they knew that they were surrounded by relatives most of whom would support them in times of need.

### Roman Catholic Church Religious Tradition.

For religious tradition, emancipation means the restoration of dignity to women through challenging some of the cultural practices that unfairly restrain women due to the domination and undue influence of men. Jesus restored the dignity of women when he permitted them to become his disciples and follow him just like his male disciples did. He did not confine them to the home, which was their traditional place among the Jewish community of his time. He allowed them to experience the uncertainty and dangers of leading an itinerant life. He liberated some of them from the yoke of illnesses that made them social outcasts of the communities in which they lived. Jesus also forgave their sins as a sign that they too were as human as men. After his resurrection, he first appeared to women to show that being a woman was no barrier to receiving God's graces. By so doing, he liberated them from the mentality that viewed women as less acceptable to God than men.

Although Paul and Tertullian sometimes seemed to retract the positive things that they taught about women, but they were sympathetic to women's liberty. Both allowed them to prophesy, and by so doing showing the church that women too had access to the spiritual gifts just like men. They encouraged widows to remain single for the purpose of their freedom because celibacy would give them the liberty and autonomy that married women of their time lacked.

Pope John Paul II worked tirelessly for the emancipation of women from male domination. He challenged men to treat women as equals at work and home. He denounced the sexual exploitation of women and children by men. He also encouraged bishops to criticize cultural practices that gave men unfair advantages over women. However, some feminist theologians think that Pope John Paul II should have gone a step further by authorizing women to participate actively in all ministries of the church such as the priesthood. Unfortunately, he did not.

For the ZCBC women emancipation means the coming together of men and women in doing duties that traditionally had been reserved for women, such as the religious education of the children. The Zimbabwe bishops encourage men to join women in educating children about prayer by taking an active part during family prayers. Emancipation also involves men. They should remove the cultural boundaries that render women unequal to men.

The RCC calls for complementarity, mutual love, respect, and equality between men and women in marriage. For religious tradition, the pursuit and achievement of the above will contribute to women's emancipation. It should be noted that women's liberation is not exclusive of men's liberty. In the same process that is intended to empower the woman, men too will be emancipated from the prejudices that lead them to view women as inferior and, therefore, failing to benefit from what women can offer. For instance, a man who systematically and constantly refuses to collaborate with his wife in making decisions that affect the family deprives his family of the wisdom of his wife. A community that forbids women from taking up leadership positions deprives the whole community of the talents of women. A church that forbids women to access priestly ordination deprives its adherents of the rich spirituality and wisdom that emanate from women.

The RCC tradition has reiterated the importance of motherhood. It has advocated the equality between men and women in all other spheres of human endeavor except in ministry and has always stressed that women and men are equal but different. The order of creation has ordained that there are certain irrevocable duties that nature has assigned either to women or men, and one such duty is the gift of motherhood. For religious tradition, women's emancipation does not mean the abandonment of the duties of motherhood that are unique to women. Emancipation of women should not undermine women's role of motherhood. For Pope John Paul II, those women who choose to stay at home as mothers should not be pressured not to do so. For religious tradition, women's emancipation means the fulfillment of the gospel message of equality, human dignity, and personal integrity of all people irrespective of gender, race, color, and nationality. Any practice, such as domestic violence, which tends to undermine the above-mentioned positive values ought to be challenged.

## Similarities and Differences

The three dialoguing partners agree that there is a need for women's emancipation. They agree that women should be respected and valued and that they should not be ill-treated. Women's dignity should be restored in situations where their dignity has been undermined. This emancipation does not take away women's divine duty and the gift of motherhood—a gift that is crucial for the continuation of the human race. The dialoguing partners agree that men and women complement each other and should assist one another.

There are also differences. Some voices of experience think that women's emancipation would bring about a completely revised outlook of the human society. Instead of emphasizing complementarity, some women want a complete reversal of duties between men and women. The RCC tradition insists that although women and men are equal, they remain different. Women cannot be equals of men in ministry, and this cannot be changed, at least, in the meantime. It emphasizes the point that there are certainly natural and fundamental aspects of women and men that cannot be interchanged. Motherhood is one example of such aspects of the natural order.

Ordinary women agree with the RCC tradition that supports the restoration of women's dignity. Culture looks at it through a different lens. For culture, the woman should be respected although women can be disciplined by moderate beating. Other forms of domestic violence such as wife restriction to the home and marital rape are not taken seriously. Hence, among the Shona, some cultural practices continue to undermine the dignity of women. Although all the three dialoguing partners support the emancipation of women, they define it differently.

## Comments

The theological conversation between religious tradition, the Shona people's experiences, and culture has both agreements and disagreements. One of the fundamental agreements is that women and men have a dignity that derives from them being human beings and that dignity should be upheld through the practice of mutual respect, fairness, and justice.

The conversation also confirmed that the institution of marriage is crucial to the continuity of the human race. Consequently, it should be protected from anything that threatens its perpetuity and integrity. The RCC refers to the family as the domestic church in which the elementary religious instructions begin. It is in families where characters of future citizens are formed. Hence, the family should be protected from anything that endangers its integrity, continuity, and peaceful existence. The RCC teaches that some cultural practices that are in line with the principles of the gospel must be upheld. But, those cultural practices that demean women's dignity by awarding more rights to men than women as the adulterated and commercialized payment of bridewealth does, should be purified by the gospel.

Although culture does not seem to be in a hurry about the transformation of the cultural practices that subjugate women, other voices think that the transformation of some cultural practices that undermine women's dignity demands urgency. Some people fear that if bridewealth is transformed or abolished, families will be destroyed because women would easily divorce abusive men, which I believe to be a reasonable concern. However, it is not good enough to protect a harmful cultural practice because of the fear of upsetting the status quo. Every transformation is painful, and unless people are willing to make some sacrifices, Shona women will continue to be exploited and oppressed. If bridewealth is abolished or regulated, will domestic violence disappear? Not at once. It takes some time for inherited patriarchal tendencies to go, but every journey of a thousand miles starts with one pace.

# Chapter 6

## The Way Forward

### Introduction

THE QUESTION TO ASK at this juncture is about what needs to be done to liberate Shona women from some cultural practices that are biased against them and are likely to cause domestic violence. It is true that in any culture and society there is no easy walk to a transformation of any kind. What people can do is to suggest strategies that can be used in such struggles. Likewise, there are some significant but not exhaustive pastoral responses that this work suggests. First, there is a need for a radical change in the cultural practices that promote domestic violence such as bridewealth. Second, anti-domestic violence activists and non-governmental organizations should be funded so that they continue to be the voice of the oppressed. Third, the government of Zimbabwe that has enacted some laws to protect women from violence should educate people about the evils of domestic violence and on ways of eradicating it. Finally, the Christian churches, which claim to be the prophetic voices of the oppressed, exploited, and marginalized should join the fight to emancipate Shona women from domestic violence and any other cultural practice that degrades them.

## Non-Governmental Organizations

### *The Musasa Project*

As has been theoretically demonstrated in chapter 1, the issue of domestic violence, particularly wife beating, is a reality among the Shona of Zimbabwe, and most people agree that something must be done to eliminate it. Non-Governmental Organizations such as the Women Action Group, the Women and Law in Southern Africa Research Project, the Zimbabwe Women Lawyers Association, Musasa Project, and others have been advocating an end to domestic violence, and for quite a long time they lobbed the Zimbabwean government to establish legislation that would make domestic violence a criminal offense. All the organizations' work is crucial to the emancipation of the women of Zimbabwe but, attempting to discuss the activities of each group is beyond the scope of this work. Consequently, only the Musasa Project will be briefly explored in this chapter because it is the most prominent group in combating domestic violence to promote and restore the dignity of women in Zimbabwe. The Musasa Project was set up in May 1988 by Jill Taylor, a psychologist, and Sheelagh Stewart, a lawyer, in Harare, Zimbabwe. Some of the Musasa Project's objectives are: to enhance the development of women in Zimbabwe; to cooperate and liaise with any groups prepared to tackle the issue of violence; to alleviate the suffering of individual women and children who have been sexually assaulted or beaten by men by providing counseling and temporary shelter, and by referring them to appropriate organizations where they can get help.[1]

The Musasa Project played a significant role in the writing of the Domestic Violence Act Chapter 5:16, No. 14/2006, which became operational in Zimbabwe on October 25, 2007. The organization carries out research on domestic violence and brings to the ordinary Zimbabweans the awareness of the evils that domestic violence causes. The project also holds awareness workshops and public education seminars for the police, health-sector workers, teachers, youth, women, and churches.[2] The Musasa Project has been instrumental in alleviating the suffering of many victims and survivors of domestic violence by providing pertinent information and temporary shelter for the victims.

Despite the inroads that the Musasa Project has made in the Shona society in its fight against domestic violence, it has also met challenges. Its leadership has been accused of spearheading the breaking up of families by promoting divorce. Some Shona people still think that the battered woman

1. This information came from a pamphlet produced by the Musasa Project in 2006.
2. Ibid.

should silently bear all the abuse she receives instead of leaving the batterer. Most people believe that all the traditional channels of settling disputes happening in marriage situations should first be exhausted before people consider the involvement of outside forces such as the Musasa Project. In the traditional Shona marriage setup, divorce was the last resort, and the elders try to avoid it as much as possible. In any spousal disputes, the elders' first instinct is to save the marriage from destruction.

In most circles of men, the Musasa Project's awareness programs are just brushed off as addressing issues that pertain only to women and have nothing to do with men. Very few men are interested in participating actively in the Musasa Project's awareness programs, perhaps due to the approach that some domestic violence activists have used in the past to disseminate their information. In some cases, they made the whole program look like it was a woman's thing that had no benefit to men at all. However, the Musasa project has since changed its outreach strategies by including men in their campaigns. Of course, some men still think that the Musasa project's programs are for women alone. The program is also perceived as anti-men since it advocates the end of wife battering, and is silent about the abuse that some men are subjected to by their wives.

Worsening the situation is the fact that there are women who belong to the old Shona school of thought that opposes any group that lobbies for equal rights for men and women. They look upon these projects as attempts by women who have failed in their marriages, and want to influence others to abandon their families so that they too may be like them. Some women who lead such projects have been accused of being failures because they are either single or windowed. And those activists who are married are also viewed with suspicion for they are sometimes accused of trying to destroy the Shona culture. They have been charged with belonging to the elite class that does not understand the basic needs of Shona women.

Some of the Musasa Project's efforts, such as providing temporary shelter to victims and survivors of domestic violence and bringing domestic violence awareness to the people of Zimbabwe, have been hampered by the lack of sufficient funds. Despite the many drawbacks that the Musasa Project encounters, the group has been instrumental in alleviating the suffering of many battered women of Zimbabwe and by so doing restoring their dignity. Currently, the project is campaigning for stiffer penalties for sexual offenders and the abolition of child marriages in Zimbabwe.

## The Government of Zimbabwe

### *Transformation of Bridewealth*

Bridewealth is an integral part of the Shona people's cultural heritage concerning marriage, and many people argue that it should be preserved by all means that are necessary. However, some of the people who practice it do not understand its history, purpose, and implications in marital relationships. This lack of knowledge may be attributed to Zimbabwe's education curriculum that does not include much of cultural studies. Although many men do not know how bridewealth came into existence and the purpose that it served when it was instituted, they are aware of the benefits that they derive from it as men. Many Shona people would agree that bridewealth has become too expensive for many people but, there has not been a platform for them to make their voices heard. Any cultural transformations require the free and informed discussions of the issues in question. So, if people are going to engage in debates that concern bridewealth, they need information about it. The government can compel all college students to study at least one course in culture to graduate so that they attain the basic knowledge of their culture.

The other challenge that needs attention concerns the discrepancies of the amount of the bridewealth charged by different families. The government has left it to the parents of the women to charge whatever amount that they want. Consequently, some parents have taken advantage of the government's indifference on how much should be paid and started charging exorbitant amounts as bridewealth. At times, it is good to trust human beings, but in matters of monetary transactions most people need legal guidance because most human beings have the proclivity to become corrupt, oppressive, and exploitive if they are left to themselves. It would be helpful if the government should stipulate guidelines on how to charge bridewealth to discourage parents from exploiting their son-in-laws. That exploitation might backfire if it leads to the groom's resentment.

The other viable but controversial solution is to abolish bridewealth altogether. It has ceased to serve the purpose for which it was established. It gives more conjugal rights to men than women. The checks and balances that were in place in the past have disintegrated. The extended family has been kicked out of the bridewealth negotiations. Yes, there are some who are convinced that bridewealth adds value to the Shona women, which some people do not agree with. Bridewealth does not add any value to Shona women. In fact, it diminishes their value. Women have value in themselves by having been created in the image of God and the humanity that they have.

There is no amount of money or cattle that can increase that value. Bridewealth adds nothing to the woman except their servitude. If men would like to thank their in-laws, they can still do that without paying bridewealth. Suppose bridewealth were abolished today, who stand to lose?

Yes, bridewealth is part of the Shona's culture, but every culture is dynamic. Any cultural practice that does not promote human dignity and freedom belongs to the museum if it cannot be updated or transformed. As has been said before, there can never be any meaningful emancipation of Shona women as long as bridewealth remains uncontrolled and corrupt as it is. Shona women cannot have both emancipation and bridewealth at the same time. If they choose bridewealth, they are likely to forego their freedom from male dominance. If they want freedom, then bridewealth has to be regulated or transformed or even abolished. The question that comes to mind is whether there is no domestic violence among cultures that do not have bridewealth? Yes, there is, but women have the option to divorce such men because they do not feel obliged to remain in such abusive marriages.

## Domestic Violence Act (Chapter 5:16)

Although before 2007 there was no specific law dealing with domestic violence in Zimbabwe, some forms of domestic violence such as sexual assault were taken seriously, and perpetrators of such crimes received prison sentences. The issuance of the Domestic Violence Act (Chapter 5:16), No. 14/2006 that became law on October 25, 2007, was the consummation of the non-governmental and government's attempts to stop domestic violence.

Apart from seeking the arrest and subsequent incarceration of perpetrators of domestic violence for not more than ten years, the law aims to establish a network of anti-domestic violence counselors and councilors that are recruited from all sectors of the Zimbabwe society. The counselors will have the task to regularly review the problem of domestic violence by disseminating information and increasing awareness; promoting research into the issue of domestic violence and the provision of services necessary to deal with all aspects of domestic violence; establishing safe-houses for the victims and survivors of domestic violence; providing support services for complainants where the perpetrator, who was the breadwinner, is imprisoned, and helping the implementation of anything that may be necessary for the fight against domestic violence.[3]

The government's efforts to put an end to domestic violence through this law will be effective to some extent. However, many factors affect its

3. *Zimbabwe Domestic Violence Act*, 1–15.

efficacy. First of all, it should be borne in mind that the purpose of this law is to protect the integrity and dignity of the Shona woman and family by discouraging all things that affect their well-being. It is not the aim of this law to break up people's families by sending perpetrators of violence to prison. However, the breakup of some marriages in the event of the husband's confinement are inevitable as a by-product of the process.

The success of this law depends on many things. The government has no difficulty in arresting perpetrators because it already has a law in place and a well-established police force. Nor does the provision of protection for the victims of domestic violence poses a problem for the government because it already has a well-trained judiciary system. The situation is different when it comes to the establishment of safe-houses for the temporal accommodation of survivors of domestic violence. The government needs money to buy food and other necessities for the people, but it does not have it. However, the drafters of this law should be applauded for being mindful of the need of support services for complainants and other dependents when a breadwinner is arrested. Here, the assumption is that the law has in mind children of school going ages who will be affected by the detention of the person who would be paying their tuition fees and living expenses. Taking into consideration the extended families among the Shona, other dependents such as parents and siblings of the perpetrators need to be given attention as well. Therefore, there is a need for adequate funds to help all those dependents. If the children fail to get food or school fees because their father has been imprisoned, they may end up on the street where they will be further abused and may become abusers themselves. The survivor of domestic violence, who in most cases is a woman who is not gainfully employed, may end up in prostitution to support herself and her family. Now that the HIV/AIDS scourge is ravaging the Shona society, this may lead to the infection of the woman, and then in the case of her illness or death, the children may end up in the streets where they may be abused like their mother.

The government of Zimbabwe has other programs that also need financings such as agriculture and the provision of food for people who need it. It also needs to fund higher education students in its universities. It pays salaries for the government departments. The point is that at present, and probably into the distant future, the government may fail to obtain the funds to support the provision of services for victims of domestic violence, and without financial support, they would then remain prisoners of domestic violence.

The promotion of research into domestic violence, which is provided for by the Act shows that the government is aware of the fact that the Act, in its present form may not have the capacity to eradicate domestic violence in Zimbabwe. It is also an acknowledgment of the fact that domestic violence is only a tip of an iceberg; it is only a symptom of hidden cultural practices, which undermine the dignity of Shona women. Such practices have led to the demeaning, subjugation, oppression, and battering of the Shona woman. There is a need for additional research into the issue. I am of the conviction that domestic violence in Zimbabwe cannot be addressed satisfactorily without revisiting the cultural practices that have provided it with fertile grounds.

Despite the shortcomings of the Domestic Violence Act, it will deter perpetrators of domestic violence to some extent although wife battering and other forms of domestic violence will likely continue. So, there is need for other complementary programs to help restore the dignity of the Shona woman and fight domestic violence, especially wife battering. The end of domestic violence will restore the dignity of Shona women, but the fight against domestic violence may not begin unless Shona people recognize the importance of restoring and upholding the dignity of women. All aspects of the Shona culture should be analyzed for the purpose of identifying their contribution to domestic violence.

## Churches

Perpetrators of domestic violence may be imprisoned, but unless the root of the problem is addressed, it may continue. All Christian churches have the responsibility to join hands with those who fight domestic violence because they have the spiritual and prophetic mandate to address both religious and social issues. In Zimbabwe the RCC, living up to its prophetic bidding, has been vocal against political violence and probably the time has come for it to speak more forcefully for the poor and oppressed of Shona society. James O'Halloran has defined the poor as, "the materially deprived, particularly those unfortunates who are so locked in a struggle for sheer survival, wondering where their next meal will come from, that they have no leisure time to devote to thoughts of spiritual enrichment. The Hebrew terms used in the Old Testament (*ani* and *dal* in particular), convey a notion of the powerlessness. The poor are the powerless ones often bereft of even the will to fight or protest. The state of powerlessness, of course, usually accompanies material deprivation."[4]

The battered women in the Shona society are among those powerless women who need the help of the RCC. It is part of the RCC's mission to

4. O'Halloran, *Signs of Hope,* 51.

preach the Good News of equality, freedom, liberation, and tranquility to the marginalized and oppressed of the Shona society—the women and children. The Fathers of the Second Vatican Council concisely acknowledged the prophetic mission of the RCC. They wrote:

> Listening to the cry of those who suffer violence and are oppressed by unjust systems and structures, and hearing the appeal of a world that by its perversity contradicts the plan of its creator, we have shared our awareness of the Church's vocation to be present in the heart of the world by proclaiming the Good News to the poor, freedom to the oppressed, and joy to the afflicted. . . . The Church, indeed, is not alone responsible for justice in the world; however, she has a proper and specific responsibility which is identified with her mission of giving witness before the world of the need for love and justice contained in the Gospel message, a witness to be carried out in Church institutions themselves and in the lives of Christians.[5]

Many domestic violence perpetrators may be jailed, but the violence will continue. The RCC should join the secular world in the fight against domestic violence through the education of Shona Catholics about the importance of love, mutuality, and justice within families, and the evils of domestic violence. This education will lead to a renewal of Shona society which will eventually lead to gender equality. Pope Paul VI asserted that the Gospel has the power to "impregnate" and "penetrate" culture to revamp cultural practices that are not in line with Gospel principles of equality and human dignity.[6] Pope John Paul II wrote: "On the other hand, the power of the Gospel everywhere transforms and regenerates. When that power enters into a culture, it is no surprise that it rectifies many of its elements. There would be no catechesis if it were the Gospel that had to change when it came into contact with the cultures."[7]

Some pastoral strategies should be set up to make sure that Shona men change their attitude towards women. This intervention of the RCC calls for the provision of multidimensional educational programs. The Church need to sponsor research into the causes of domestic violence, especially wife battering, and that research should be followed by the issuance of a pastoral letter.

5. Flannery, ed., *Vatican Council II, More Post Conciliar Documents*, 1971.

6. Paul VI, *Evangelii Nuntiandi*, 20; Flannery, ed., *Vatican Council II, More Post Conciliar Documents*, 719.

7. John Paul II, *Catechesis in Our Time*, October 16, 1979, 53; Flannery, ed., *Vatican Council II, More Post Conciliar Documents*, 762.

## *Pastoral Letter*

The RCC in Zimbabwe should welcome the government's suggestion that is provided in the Domestic Violence Act (Chapter 5:16) No. 14/2006 that says that research into domestic violence should be encouraged and supported. Pope John Paul II also urged the Bishops of Africa to establish special commissions to study women's problems.[8] The RCC is one of the Christian denominations that has many highly educated ministers that are capable of carrying out research in areas such as domestic violence. This research may be done by qualified individual priests, laypersons or commissions set up by the bishops to look into the issue of domestic violence, its causes, and the ways by which it may be eradicated.

After the researchers or commissions have gathered sufficient and relevant information regarding domestic violence, the bishops may write a pastoral letter addressing that issue. Similar pastoral letters have been written elsewhere. In 2002, the United States Conference of Catholic Bishops wrote a pastoral letter entitled *When I Call for Help: A Pastoral Response to Domestic Violence Against Women*, in which they addressed issues surrounding woman dignity and domestic violence and gave their pastoral response.[9] A pastoral letter is different from an ordinary letter because it carries the teaching authority of the pastors of the church.

In many parishes in Zimbabwe, pastoral letters are read publicly in churches, usually immediately after the Sunday service. Most parishioners have the responsibility to stay in church after the Mass so that they may listen to the pastoral letter being read. They may discuss the contents of the letter in small groups. This active participation by church-goers will fulfill the spirit of *Evangelii Nuntiandi,* which calls upon all Christians to be witnesses of the Good News. It would benefit not only the Christian community but also the whole world.[10] According to Barbara A. Stolz, family violence is a problem, which the church at all levels has a responsibility to address because of the church's concern for human life, social justice, and its historical role as a sanctuary for those people whose well-being is threated and endangered.[11]

8. John Paul II, *The African Synod Comes Home: A Simplified Text,* 121.

9. USCCB, *When I Call for Help.*

10. Paul VI, *Evangelii Nuntiandi,* 1 and 21.

11. Stolz, *Violence in the Family,* 1.

## On-going Formation

Methods of evangelization and religious education should constantly be revised to suit the ever-changing needs, wants, and environment of the community.[12] John L. Elias is of the opinion that there are bound to be demographic and family changes, among others, which have an impact on the methods used to impart religious education to both adults and youth. He is of the opinion that if adult religious education is to be truly effective, it must "show an awareness of patterns, cycles, and problems that families face in contemporary society."[13] The Shona society has gone through a great deal of economic and social changes and, therefore, religious education should be mindful and relevant to the people's context. The ever changing contexts of the Christians requires a constant revisit to the methods of evangelization. The issue of domestic violence requires everyone to be educated about it.

So, after the Zimbabwe Bishops complete the writing of the pastoral letter, it would be the priests' duty and responsibility to read and explain its contents to their parishioners. To prepare priests for the crucial task of changing the mindset of Christians they may attend workshops that are facilitated by the researchers and other domestic violence activists. Those workshops will deepen their knowledge and awareness of women dignity and domestic violence in parishes. Priests require that knowledge because sometimes some of their parishioners are victims or survivors of domestic violence. These workshops could also be attended by religious sisters, brothers, and catechists who have always worked tirelessly for the welfare of the people of God.

The priest is a paramount person in the restoration and upholding of the dignity of the marginalized and the fight against domestic violence because most priests have the authority and respect that is needed to influence parishioners. The Roman Catholic priest has the availability of the pulpit. The priest may choose to preach against domestic violence on suitable occasions such as weddings. One of the RCC's missions, "preferential option for the marginalized," is not only about the materially poor, but the powerless—the battered woman. Besides preaching, the priest may be able to organize workshops on domestic violence at the parish level. The priest may invite experts to address the people so that what he preaches would be affirmed by other experts.

Priests might also write reflections in their parish bulletins or newspapers, which would reinforce what the bishops would have written in their

12. Paul VI, *Evangelii Nuntiandi*, 3; Flannery, ed., *Vatican Council II, More Post Conciliar Documents*, 712.

13. Elias, *The Foundations and Practice of Adult Religious Education*, 45.

pastoral letter. The objective would be to raise awareness about the evils of domestic violence. Priests together with other religious education teachers could then plan diocesan congresses for men and women.

Biblical feminist hermeneutics can be utilized in the fight to restore Shona women's dignity. Priests can deliberately opt for the oppressed in their homilies. They can challenge patriarchal practices that subjugate women. They may as well employ biblical feminist interpretational methods in their preaching. Biblical passages that denigrate women can be interpreted in a way that empowers women. Cultural practices that are not in line with the principles of the gospel may be challenged. Women may be encouraged to take up church leadership positions. Abused women should be respected and ministered to in a compassionate way. It also calls for the retraining of the catechists, most of whom are barely catechized.

## Small Christian Communities

Small Christian Communities (SCC) have been operative in Zimbabwe for a long time and have been very influential in the spiritual and religious formation of Catholics in Zimbabwe. James O'Halloran has defined "Small Christian Communities" as a group of Christians consisting of about eight and not more than thirty members who are usually related to a specific area or neighborhood.[14] Margaret Hebblethwaite has defined the SCC as "the basic cell of the Church" which is for everyone, and which brings together faith and life through social analysis, theological reflection, and the pursuit of action.[15] The communities include sharing of love and reading of the word of God contextually. According to Thomas Maney, the SCC should consist of entire families, adults, and youth who intend to foster a growth of faith through interpersonal relationships.[16]

Their activities involve praying together, reading and sharing of the word of God, preparation for Sunday liturgy, and visiting the sick. They are mostly led by women since women constitute the majority of SCC members. Unfortunately, SCC in Zimbabwe have not been involved in discussions of poverty, human dignity, and violence, most probably due to lack of awareness of how to deal with those issues. Small Christian Communities can give people an opportunity to learn about human dignity, faith, and social issues. Although in Zimbabwe, SCC have thriving programs, they need trained facilitators who have religious and social issues knowledge. Since

14. O'Halloran, *Small Christian Communities,* 50.

15. Hebblethwaite, *Base Communities,* 15–19.

16. Maney, *Basic Communities,* 2.

members of a SCC live in the same locality, they know the problems that are afflicting their members. Consequently, they can influence and bring about a transformation of their communities by challenging each member to grow in faith and love. James O'Halloran has warned that the communities should realize that growth is gradual and that it can neither be "unduly rushed nor unduly delayed. . . It involves taking people where they are, challenging them to grow, and striving to create the environment of love and acceptance that makes growth possible."[17]

The SCC provides a conducive environment for spiritual and religious growth because the leaders know each member's educational and emotional needs. Victims of domestic violence may be encouraged to tell their stories which in most cases the community already knows. The perpetrators may be challenged to desist from their destructive behavior since the community may already know the men who batter their wives. The SCC need not change their procedure of group meeting, but they need to take every opportunity to raise awareness among their members of the evils of domestic violence. They could be encouraged to dedicate certain periods of the year to praying for victims and perpetrators of domestic violence and raising awareness of the need to uphold woman dignity.

## Comments

The church is the best starting place for any meaningful change of mind, heart, and attitude. It has the personnel, prophetic mission, and responsibility to do that. The church has a willing audience whose goal is to transform their lives by imitating the way of Jesus Christ. The audience include both perpetrators and victims or survivors, and one homily can reach both sides. The church has the infrastructure in which to conduct workshops and conferences. It has schools in which topics such as human dignity may be included into the school's curriculum. Students may establish clubs that aim at challenging domestic violence. Some people have argued that the church is not beyond reproach with regards to moral uprightness—that is true. But, the church has never claimed to be the home of saints, but of people who strive to be better. Any revolution that starts in the church has a better chance of having a following because most adherents trust their pastors.

17. O'Halloran, *Small Christian Communities*, 65.

# Conclusion

IT HAS BEEN SAID that the family is the "Domestic Church" and as such it is a critical constituent of the RCC and any other Christian denomination, both now and in the future. The future of any religious tradition is molded by the character, beliefs, values, and traditions of the people who uphold them. Likewise, future families are shaped by the worldviews of the present families. Happy, just, loving, and peaceful families are more likely to give us friendly, loving, just, and happy families, society, and church in the future. Domestic violence does not promote a healthy future for the human society because it attacks and disturbs the foundation of the future church or society—the family. Consequently, violence in the family is likely to produce a violent society. It would be hard for people to learn peaceful ways of resolving relational differences if they are accustomed to seeing their role models using violence to settle such differences. According to Barbara A. Stolz, "Since the family is the primary environment in which we learn to relate to others, violence in the family does have consequences for the larger society."[1] To eradicate violence in our communities, we should start from the smallest cell of the society—the family.

Domestic violence is ubiquitous and secretive, and therefore, not easy to completely eradicate. That challenge does not matter much. What matters is what people do to discourage and hold accountable those who have a proclivity to use violence to resolve disputes. Instead of just dealing with its consequences, such as arresting perpetrators and rehabilitating victims and survivors, it is also imperative that any society that wants to eradicate domestic violence should address its root causes. Among the Shona, one of those causes is the cultural practice of bridewealth that tends to empower Shona men at the expense of women. Domestic violence undermines the dignity and rights of the Shona women and leads to family instability by causing fear, suffering, injury, or even death of women.

---

1. Stolz, *Violence in the Family*, 2.

Although non-governmental organizations and the Government of Zimbabwe have been working so hard to minimize domestic violence, other players such as churches should step in to augment those efforts. This call does not intend to trivialize the work that some Christian groups have been doing to empower women in Zimbabwe. But, its intention is to encourage more players to come aboard. It is plausible that the Government has stepped up efforts to eliminate domestic violence by providing people with the legal framework in which to operate, but it should be everyone's business to make it work. It should be noted that domestic violence does not die easily because it is inscribed in people's blood, worldview, and mentality. A worldview does not change within a short period—a lot of time, conducive environment, and effort are needed. The wretched economic situation in Zimbabwe makes life even more challenging for the unemployed women, some of whom are compelled to rely on their gainfully employed husbands for sustenance. That dependence might lead to the misuse of power that results in the abuse of women by some men.

This book calls for a metanoia, which requires the transformation of some Shona cultural practices. However, it should be remembered that any change of attitude, heart, and mind is not an easy task. It is a gradual and onerous process that demands undivided commitment, radical reorientation, and perseverance from all the concerned parties. The transformation of cultural practices is even more complicated because culture is considered to be sacrosanct by many people. For some people, culture should never be challenged because it is their heritage and it gives them their identity. But, there are also people who argue that if any cultural practice undermines the dignity, integrity, and rights of the people, it has to be discarded or transformed to suit the new context and aspirations of that people. Culture is dynamic and should serve humanity rather than having humanity serving culture. A cultural practice that tends to enslave the people who practice it has lost its relevance. The global village in which we live, and the Christian faith that some of us confess, invite us to reexamine some of our cultural practices to assess if they are compatible with the global ethic and the principles of the gospel of Jesus Christ, respectively.

Domestic violence is evil and because of that, it should be stopped. Ordinarily, everyone has a role to play in the fight against domestic violence. But, Christians, by their prophetic mission, have a special role in this struggle. The gospel that Christians preach empowers them to opt for the poor, powerless, abused, and oppressed. The churches in Zimbabwe must complement the efforts of those people who are already working for the empowerment and emancipation of our women by denouncing those tendencies that undermine the important roles that women play in the

Zimbabwean society. Churches are the best starting point to transform any cultural practices and restore the dignity and humanity of any subjugated people because they do have the personnel, platform, and the prophetic authority to do that. Although this work was written from a Roman Catholic perspective, it applies to all religions, and they should be involved in combating domestic violence.

Perhaps, the question to ask at this point is: "Is a violence-free Shona society desirable and achievable?" Such a question may sound too simplistic, but there are some Shona men who would want to maintain some cultural practices because they give them advantages over women. However, to the majority of Zimbabweans, a society that is free from any violence is desirable. Its complete achievability, though elusive, is something that we strive and hope for as a people. Certainly, it is the appropriate attitude of all who profess their allegiance to Christ. Zoe-Obianga has put it thus: "Commitment to Christ requires the liberation of African women. They should no longer be slaves: not of uncomprehending and intransigent husbands and brothers, nor of retrogressive society, nor of alienating Church structures."[2]

Are the Christian churches in Zimbabwe able to rise to the task? Absolutely. They have a prophetic mandate and moral imperative to challenge negative cultural practices that undermine the dignity of Shona women. It is true that in any given undertaking there is bound to be opposition and perhaps limited success but, some significant benefits will be reaped, eventually. The transformation of people's faith or tradition is never the work of human hands alone, but it is also the work of the Holy Spirit, through the fragile hands and works of people.

It should be noted that this project does not claim to give the panacea for all women oppression and suffering in Zimbabwe. What it does is to name the problem and create the platform for people to talk about it. So, this book should not be taken as catechetical truth but as one of the lone voices of those calling in the wilderness, saying, "revisit your cultural, religious, political, economic, and social practices, examine them openly and meticulously, and transform what calls for transformation." It's our culture, we should be free to talk about it without the fear of ostracization, and even transform it if need be.

Are the Shona women treated worse than other women in the world? I do not think so. As a teacher of world religions, I have come to realize that the emancipation of women from oppressive cultural, political, economic, religious, and social structures is a worldwide struggle. The challenge that oppressive cultural practices pose is that they are evidently evil

---

2. Zoe-Obianga, "The Role of Women in Present Day Africa," 148.

to the outsider, but good and normal to the insider. Many outsiders will be devastated to read about the experiences of Shona women, Muslim women, Rastafari women, Jewish women, Christian women, Hindu women, Jain women, and many others. But, most insiders see nothing wrong with the manner in which they treat their women—it is their tradition. When I came to America I was taken aback and discouraged to learn that some American women do not earn equal salaries as their male workmates with the same qualifications and job experiences. In Zimbabwe, that dehumanizing policy ended in 1980, when the country earned its independence from Britain. I was also shocked to learn that American women do not get the three months paid maternity leave that I had always taken as a given and for granted in Zimbabwe.

This reminds me of a class discussion that we had in one of my Religious Quest classes. The class was exploring the general benefits and setbacks that Muslim and American women have. One of the male Muslim student expressed his dissatisfaction with the way American women are treated. For him, American women suffer several setbacks. They have to compete with men in the job market and at the same time bear and take care of the children. They work the same number of hours as men, yet, some of them receive lower remuneration than men. They are caught up in horrible traffic congestions as they drive to and from home or one job to another. For him, women should not be treated like that because that is disrespectful and demeaning to the many sacrifices that they make for the good of the society. Women should be treated like queens—staying at home and being chauffer driven when they go out shopping. But, the American students viewed the same as freedom.

That's how culture influences our perspectives. We interpret our experiences through our cultural lenses, and consequently, we tend to condemn and demonize any practice or belief that is different from our own. We tend to see the splinter that is in another person's eye, but failing to see the log that is in our own eyes. The goal of this project is to encourage each cultural group to perform introspection and discernment, identify those not so good practices that exploit and subjugate women, and then transform them. This work is not only about Shona women, but all women who are impeded to achieve their full humanity and potentiality by patriarchal, cultural, economic, political, and social practices that tend to exploit, oppress, and subjugate women in the world.

# Bibliography

Anderson, Herbert. "Between Rhetoric and Reality: Women and Men as Equal Partners in Home, Church, and the Marketplace." In *Mutuality Matters: Faith, Family, and Just Love*, edited by Herbert Anderson et al., 67–82. Oxford: Rowman and Littlefield, 2004.

Bancroft, Lundy. *Why Does He Do That? Inside the Minds of Angry and Controlling Men.* New York: Putnam's Sons, 2002.

Barnes, Timothy, D. *Tertullian: A Historical and Literary Study.* Oxford: Clarendon, 1985.

Bassler, M Jouette. "1 Corinthians." In *The Women's Bible Commentary*, edited by Newsom and Ringe, 557–65. London: SPCK, 1992.

Baumert, Norbert. *Woman and Man in Paul: Overcoming a Misunderstanding.* Collegeville, MN: Liturgical, 1996.

Bhebe, Ngwabi. *Christianity and Traditional Religion in Western Zimbabwe.* London: Longman, 1979.

Boldrey, Richard, and Joyce Boldrey. *Chauvinist or Feminist? Paul's View of Women.* Grand Rapids: Baker, 1976.

Bourdillon, Michael M. *The Shona Peoples.* Gweru: Mambo, 1987.

Bray, Gerald L. *Holiness and the Will of God: Perspectives on the Theology of Tertullian.* Atlanta: John Knox, 1979.

Byrne, Brendan. *Paul and the Christian Woman.* Collegeville, MN: Liturgical, 1989.

Chigwedere, Aenias S. *Lobola—The Pros and Cons.* Harare: Apex Holdings, 1982.

Clark, Elizabeth, A., *Women in the Early Church.* Wilmington, DE: Glazier, 1983.

Colson, Elizabeth. *Marriage and the Family among the Tonga of Northern Rhodesia.* Manchester: Manchester University Press, 1958.

Cooke, Bernard, and Gary Macy. *A History of Women and Ordination.* Vol. 1, *The Ordination of Women in Medieval Context.* London: Scarecrow, 2002.

Crowell, Nancy A., and Ann W. Burgess, eds. *Understanding Violence against Women.* Washington, DC: National Academy, 1996, 9.

Dalton, Louis. "Catholic High Schools: Organizing the Religion." In *Youth Ministry: A Book of Readings*, edited by Michael Warren, 93–94. New York: Paulist, 1977.

Daneel, Marthinus L. *Old and New in Southern Shona Independent Churches.* Vol. 1, *Background and Rise of the Major Movements.* Herderstraat, Netherlands: Mouton, 1971.

Davidson, Terry. *Conjugal Crime: Understanding and Changing the Wife Beating.* New York: Hawthorn, 1978.

Davies, Miranda, compiler. *Women and Violence: Realities and Responses Worldwide.* London: Zed, 1994.

Dewalt, M. Kathleen, and R. Billie Dewalt. *Participant Observation: A Guide for Fieldworkers.* New York: Altamira, 2002.

Elias, John L. *The Foundations and Practice of Adult Religious education.* Malabar, FL: Krieger, 1982.

Evans-Pritchard, E. E. *The Position of Women in Primitive Societies and Other Essays in Social Anthropology.* New York: Free, 1965.

Fitzmyer, A. Joseph. *Luke the Theologian: Aspects of His Teaching.* New York: Paulist: 1989.

Flannery, Austin, ed. *Vatican Council II, More Post Conciliar Documents.* Boston: St. Paul, 1982.

Fox, Robin. *Kinship and Marriage: An Anthropological Perspective.* Cambridge: Cambridge University Press, 1967.

Freire, Paulo. *Pedagogy of the Oppressed.* Translated by Myra Bergman Ramos. New York: Herder and Herder, 1972.

Freyne, Sean. Galilee, *Jesus and the Gospels: Literary Approaches and Historical Investigations.* Philadelphia: Fortress, 1988.

Gelfand, Michael. *The Genuine Shona.* Gweru: Mambo, 1973.

Gelles, Richard J. *Family Violence,* 2nd Edition. Newbury Park, CA: Sage, 1987.

Gillman, M. Florence. *Women Who Knew Paul.* Collegeville, MN: Liturgical, 1992.

Goody, Jack and S.J. Tambiah, *Bridewealth and Dowry.* London: Cambridge University Press, 1973.

Grant, Michael. *Jesus: An Historian's Review of the Gospels.* New York: Scribner,1977.

Green, Andrew. *Divorce for Women: A Practical Handbook.* Pietermaritzburg, South Africa: Ashanti, 1989.

Gryson, Roger. *The Ministry of Women in the Early Church.* Translated by Jean Laporte and Mary L. Hall. Collegeville, MN: Liturgical, 1976.

Hastings, Adrian. *Christian Marriage in Africa: A Report.* London: SPCK, 1973.

Hebblethwaite, Margaret. *Base Communities: An Introduction.* Mahwah, NJ: Paulist, 1994.

Hill, Brennan. *Jesus the Christ: Contemporary Perspectives.* Mystic, CT: Twenty-third, 1991.

Hoffman, Daniel, L. *The Status of Women and Gnosticism in Irenaeus and Tertullian.* Lewiston, NY: Mellen, 1995.

Holleman, F. Johan. *The Pattern of Hera Kinship.* London: Oxford University Press, 1949.

———. *Shona Customary Law.* London: Oxford University Press, 1952.

House, H. Wayne. "Paul, Women, and Contemporary Evangelical Feminism." *Bibliotheca Sacra* 136, no. 541 (1979) 40–53.

Huels, John H. *The Pastoral Companion: A Canon Law Handbook for Catholic Ministry.* Revised, Updated, and Expanded. Quincy, IL: Quincy University Press, 1995.

Jacobson, Neil, and John Gottan. *When Men Batter Women: New Insights into Ending Abusive Relationships.* New York: Simon and Schuster, 1998.

John Paul II. *The African Synod Comes Home: A Simplified Text.* Nairobi: Paulines, 1995.

John Paul II. *Mulieris Dignitatem.* Rome: Libreria Editrice Vaticana, 1988.

John Paul II. *The Church in Africa: And Its Evangelizing Mission towards the Year 2000.* Washington DC: USCC, 2000.

Johnson Elizabeth, A. *Consider Jesus: Waves of Renewal in Christology*. New York: Crossroad, 1990.

Kakar, Suman. *Domestic Abuse, Public Policy / Criminal Justice: Approaches towards Child, Spousal and Elderly Abuse*. San Francisco: Austin and Winfield, 1998.

Keener, S. Craig. *Paul, Women and Wives: Marriage and Women's Ministry in the Letters of Paul*. Peabody, MA: Hendrickson, 1992.

Kisembo, Benezeri et al., *African Christian Marriage*. Nairobi: Paulines, 1998.

Kleingeld, Pauline. "Just Love? Marriage and the Question of Justice." In *Mutuality Matters: Faith, Family, and Just Love*, edited by Herbert Anderson et al., 23–42. Oxford: Rowman and Littlefield, 2004.

Kuper, Adam. *Wives for Cattle: Bridewealth and Marriage in Southern Africa*. London: Routledge, 1982.

LaPorte, Jean. *The Role of Women in Early Christianity*. New York: Mellen, 1982.

Leddy, M. Margaret. "Domestic Violence: A Pastoral Response Guide." MA thesis, Catholic Theological Union, 2004.

Mabhawu, Timothy. *Zimbabwe Parliamentary Debates*. 2006.

Mair, Lucy. *Marriage*. London: Penguin, 1971.

Maney, Thomas. *Basic Communities: A Practical Guide for Renewing Neighborhood Churches*. Minneapolis: Winston, 1984.

Manning, Joanna. *Is the Pope Catholic: A Woman Confronts Her Church*. New York: Crossroad, 1999.

May, Melanie, A. *Women and Church: The Challenge of Ecumenical Solidarity in an Age of Alienation*. Grand Rapids: Eerdmans, 1991.

Mawere, Munyaradzi, and Annastancia Mbindi Mawere. "The Changing Philosophy of African Marriage: The Relevance of the Shona Customary Marriage Practice of Kukumbira." *Journal of African Studies and Development* 2, no. 9 (2010) 224–33.

Mbiti, John S. *African Religions and Philosophy*. New York: Doubleday, 1970.

McBrien, Richard, P. "An Ecclesiology for Women and Men." In *Women in the Church*, edited by Madonna Kolbenschlag, 19–30. Washington DC: Pastoral, 1987.

McGrath, M. Albertus. *Women and the Church*. New York: Image, 1976.

Meskeen, El Matta. *Women: Their Rights and Obligations in Social and Religious Life in the Early Church*. Cairo: Monastery of St Macarius, 1984.

Mlambo, Alois S. *A History of Zimbabwe*. New York: Cambridge University Press, 2014.

Murape, Wenceslous. *The Herald*, Harare, May 29, 2007.

Murphree, W. Marshall. *Christianity and the Shona*. London: University of London, 1969.

Musasa Project. *Domestic Violence (Prevention and Protection of Victims) Bill*. 2003.

Musasa Project. *Regional Skills Clinic*. Harare, November 25–27, 1998.

Mvududu, Sarah, and Patricia McFadden. *Reconceptualizing the Family in a Changing Southern Africa Environment*. Harare: WLSA Research Trust, 2001.

Ngubane, Harriet. "The Consequences for Women of Marriage Payments in a Society with Patrilineal Descent." In *Transformations of African Marriages*, edited by David Parkin and David Nyamwaya, 173–81. Manchester: Manchester University Press for the International African Institute, 1987.

O'Day, R. Gail. "Acts." In *The Women's Bible Commentary*, edited by Carol A. Newsom and Sharon H. Ringe, 305–12. London: SPCK, 1992.

O'Halloran, James. *Signs of Hope: Developing Small Christian Communities*. Maryknoll, NY: Orbis, 1991.

———. *Small Christian Communities: A Pastoral Companion*. Dublin: Columba, 1996.

Obach, E. Robert, with Albert Kirk. *A Commentary on the Gospel of Luke*. Mahwah: Paulist, 1986.

Oduyoye, Mercy Amba. *Introducing African Women's Theology*. Cleveland: Pilgrim with Sheffield, 2001.

Okure, Teresa. "Contemporary Perspectives on Women in the Bible." In *Word of God in Africa*, vol. 9 of *The Bulletin for Biblical Pastoral Ministry in the IMBISA Region*, edited by Ignatius Chidavaenzi and Krystian Traczyk, 7–15. Women in the Bible. Harare: Biblical Pastoral Ministry, 2000.

Paschal, Harold, J. Paschal. *The Secret Scandal: Battered Wives*. Canfield, OH: Alba House, 1977.

Perrin, Norman. *Rediscovering the Teachings of Jesus*. New York: Harper & Row, 1967.

Professional Education Taskforce on Family Violence. *Family violence: everybody's business, somebody's life*, Leichhardt, Sydney: Federation, 1994.

Quasten, Johannes. *Patrology: The Ante-Nicene Literature after Irenaeus*. Westminster, MD: Newman, 1953.

Radcliffe-Brown, A. R. "Introduction." In *African Systems of Kinship and Marriage*, edited by A. R. Radcliffe-Brown and Daryl Forde, 1–85. London: Oxford University Press, for The International African Institute, 1967.

Rankin, David. *Tertullian and the Church*. Cambridge: Cambridge University Press, 1995.

Rayner, William. *The Tribe and its Successors: An Account of African Traditional Life and European Settlement in Southern Rhodesia*. 1st ed. London: Faber and Faber, 1962.

Reid, E. Barbara. *Choosing the Better Half? Women in the Gospel of Luke*. Collegeville, MN: Liturgical, 1996.

Ruether, Radford Rosemary. *Women and Roman Catholic Christianity*. Washington DC: Catholics for a Free Choice, 2000.

Schaberg, Jane. "Luke." In *The Women's Bible Commentary*, edited by Carol A. Newsom and Sharon H. Ringe, 275–92. London: SPCK, 1992.

Schineller, Peter. *A Handbook of Inculturation*. New York: Paulist, 1990.

Schneider, Elizabeth M. *Battered Women and Feminist Lawmaking*. London: Yale University Press, 2000.

Seim, Kaelsen Turid. "The Gospel of Luke." In *Searching the Scriptures*, edited by Elizabeth Schussler Fiorenza, 2:720–762. New York: Crossroad, 1994.

Sewall, P. Rebecca, et al., eds. *State Responses to Domestic Violence: Current Status and Needed Improvements*. Washington, DC: Institute for Women, Law and Development, 1996.

Schmidt, Elizabeth. *Peasants, Traders, and Wives, Shona Women in the History of Zimbabwe, 1870–1939*. Portsmouth, NH: Heinemann, 1992.

Schüssler Fiorenza, Elizabeth. *In Memory of Her: A Feminist Theological Reconstruction of Christian Origins*. 10th anniv. ed. New York: Crossroad, 1983.

Shoko, Tabona. *Karanga Indigenous Religion in Zimbabwe: Health and Well-Being*. Hampshire, UK: Ashgate, 2007.

Shorter, Aylward. *African Culture and the Christian Church: An Introduction to Social and Pastoral Anthropology*. New York: Orbis, 1974.

Ssenyondo, B. John. "Ganda Customary Marriage and Christian Marriage: A Search for a Relationship." MA thesis, Catholic Theological Union, Chicago, 1991.

Stapleton, Jean, and Richard Bright. *Equal Marriage*. Nashville: Abingdon, 1976.

Stewart, Sheelagh. "Working the System: Sensitizing the Police to the Plight of Women in Zimbabwe." In *Musasa Project Pamphlet*, May 5, 2001.

Stolz, Barbara, A. *Violence in the Family: A National Concern, A Church Concern.* Washington DC: United States Catholic Conference, 1979.

Taylor, Gerard. "Recent Developments in Canonical Legislation, Jurisprudence and Church Practice: Declaration of Nullity and Dissolution Cases." In *Church and Marriage in Eastern Africa*, edited by Aylward Shorter, 31–61. Eldoret, Kenya: AMECEA Research Department, 1975.

Thurston, B. Bonnie. *The Widows: A Ministry in the Early Church.* Minneapolis: Fortress, 1989.

Uchem, Rose, and N. Uchem. *Beyond Veiling: A Response to the Issues in Women's Experiences of Subjugation in African Christian Cultures.* Enugu, Nigeria: Snaap, 2002.

USCCB. *When I Call for Help: A Pastoral Response to Domestic Violence against Women.* Washington DC: USCCB, 2002.

USCCB. *The Genius of Women.* Washington, DC: USCCB, 1997.

Waits, Kathleen. *Battered Women and Their Children: Lessons from One Woman's Story,* Houston: Houston Law Review, 1998.

Walker, E. Lenore. *The Battered Woman.* New York: Harper & Row, 1979.

Warren, Michael. "Youth Ministry: An Overview." In *Youth Ministry: A Book of Readings*, edited by Michael Warren, 3–11. New York: Paulist, 1977.

Whitehead, D. James, and E. Evelyn Whitehead. *Method in Ministry: Theological Reflection and Christian Ministry.* Chicago: Sheed and Ward, 1995.

Yates, Kyle M., Jr., ed. "African Traditional Religion." In *The Religious World: Communities of Faith*, edited by Kyle M. Yates Jr., 43. New York: Macmillan, 1988.

Young Serenity, ed. *An Anthology of Sacred Texts by and about Women.* London: Pandora, 1993.

ZCBC, EFZ, and ZCC. *The Zimbabwe We Want: Towards a National Vision for Zimbabwe: A Discussion Document.* September 15, 2006.

ZCBC, EFZ, and ZCC. *The Zimbabwe We Want: "Towards a National Vision for Zimbabwe": A Discussion Document.* Harare, September 15, 2006.

ZCBC. *A Call to Metanoia: Listen to the Inner Voice.* Harare, March 2003.

ZCBC. *Christian Marriage and Family Life.* 1984.

ZCBC. *Male and Female He Created Them.* 1996.

Zimbabwe. *Customary Marriage Act* [Chapter 5:07].

Zimbabwe. *Domestic Violence Act* [Chapter 5:16] No. 14/2006.

Zoe-Obianga, Rose. "The Role of Women in Present Day Africa." In *Africa Theology en Route*, edited by Kofi Appiah-Kubi and Sergio Torres, 145–49. Maryknoll, NY: Orbis, 1979.

# Index of Authors